Mc

It's Okay to YELL at God...

I have been where Eric Miller has been: in that place where prayers for recovery turn into prayers for miracles... prayers that ultimately went unanswered when my son Andrew died at the age of three. In this book, Eric describes his own struggles with faith, life, and the death of a son seemingly taken before his time. You will be encouraged as you read about his journey of grief, a journey that so many of us have taken, a journey that can lead to hope if allowed to.

—**MARK RYPIEN,** Super Bowl MVP Quarterback
Founder, Rypien Foundation

Eric Miller has written a book that nobody wants to write but everyone wants to read. In vivid and candid detail he opens up about the darkest hours of his life and his struggle with God after the loss of a child. His story will bring you to tears and then wipe them away several times over as his heartbreak, hope, and healing are described. Simply put, this is a story that must be told. I assure you that it will inspire you to trust God more, especially in the hardest of times.

—**NATHAN RECTOR**
Senior Pastor, Valley Real Life

I have to tell you that your book left me speechless. Speechless in a good way, of course. I finished it early yesterday and it was like I couldn't put into words how much it touched me and how much I needed to read those words of encouragement at this point in my life. I haven't lost a child or gone through anything close to what you've been through, but there are many things in life that you grieve without knowing that's what's happening.

—**MONYA MOLLOHAN**
Art Director

Eric Miller is a unique and exceptional person who suffered an inexplicable tragedy. "It's Okay to Yell at God" brings to print the distilled wisdom he gained from his painful journey to master his life after his son's death. From my vantage point as a small part of his life I witnessed the value of his viewpoint before and after the loss of Micah. Due to the inevitability of tragedy in our lives this book is a gift to all.

—**BILLY O. BARCLAY, M.D.**, Medical Director of Addiction Medicine, Wexner Medical Center, The Ohio State University, Diplomate American Board of Psychiatry and Neurology, with Added Qualifications in Addiction Psychiatry, Diplomate American Board of Adolescent Psychiatry

Eric Miller has given us a beautifully written, intensely personal, and hands-on practical journey through grief. Best of all, Jesus Christ is at the center of the book. You will cry, you will laugh, you will think, you will change. And you will learn how to grieve.

—**DAVID E. CLARKE, PH.D.**, Christian psychologist, speaker, and author of I Don't Want a Divorce, www.davidclarkeseminars.com

The greatest tragedy one may face is the loss of a child. Yet all of us must deal with crisis and loss during our lives. Eric Miller has given us insight on how he and his wife coped with the sudden loss of their child and came out changed but whole. A spiritual and inspirational survival guide on traversing the grief process.

—**JUDY FELGENHAUER, MD,**
Pediatric Oncologist

It's Okay to YELL at God...

And Other Life Changing Discoveries Made on My Journey of Grief

ERIC MILLER

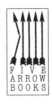

FIVE
ARROW
BOOKS

F I V E
A R R O W
B O O K S

Copyright © 2014 by Eric Miller and Five Arrow Books

Five Arrow Books, the imprint of Eric Miller

PO Box 424, Veradale, WA 99037

Permissions

Scripture quotations are from The Holy Bible, English Standard Version® (ESV®), copyright © 2001 by Crossway, a publishing ministry of Good News Publishers. Used by permission. All rights reserved.

Madeleine L'Engle quote copyright © 1996 by Crosswicks, Ltd. Reprinted courtesy of Edward Necarsulmer IV Literary Management LLC.

The Miracle of Conception article copyright © 2013 Kidspot.com.au. Reprinted with permission of Kidspot.

What About Bob? quotes copyright © 1991 Touchstone Pictures. Used by permission of Disney Enterprises, Inc.

Publisher's Cataloging-in-Publication Data

Miller, Eric Ryan.
     It's okay to yell at God— : and other life changing discoveries made on my journey of grief / Eric Miller.
          pages cm
     ISBN: 978-0-9912993-0-0 (pbk.)
     ISBN: 978-0-9912993-1-7 (e-book)
     1. Grief. 2. God (Christianity). 3. Children—Death—Psychological aspects. 4. Parents—Psychology . I. Title.
     BF575.G7 .M5299 2014
     155.9`37085—dc23
          2013957199

Cover design and typesetting by Authorsupport.com.

Photographs by Tiffany Vakaloloma at Inspirations by Tiffany.

Five Arrow Books logo design by Saralynn Downing.

Printed in the United States of America

Dedication

To Jennamae, my best friend and wife. We have walked this journey of life together for over fourteen years now. I don't know where the remainder of the journey will take us, or how many steps we have left, but I can't imagine walking it with anyone else.

To Micah, Owen, Amelia, Peyton, and Ava – our five arrows. My simple prayer is this: that from us you will take the best and leave the rest, that once you leave our hands, you will find yourself flying far and true.

TABLE OF CONTENTS

CHAPTER 1

Come Walk With Me

I know how Pharaoh felt.

I'm sorry, that's too vague. Let me be more specific. I know how Pharaoh – the one in the Biblical account of the exodus, the one who stubbornly refused Moses's pleas, the one who had seen nine various plagues descend upon his land – felt when the tenth and final plague visited his household.

When his firstborn son died.

My own son, firstborn to my wife and me, died in 2003

at the tender young age of sixteen months. We had no other children of our own at that time. He was our world, our first-born, quite literally the love of our lives.

Granted, I do not relate with Pharaoh in all manners of his grief experience. My son's death wasn't caused by any hardened heart or great sin on my part (although there was someone who dared postulate that; more on that later). And I certainly do not recall having boils fester upon my skin, frogs more numerable than the sands of the earth in my house, swarms of locusts visit my yard, nor an entire people enslaved to do my personal bidding.

But the end results – the death of a deeply cherished child, and the subsequent soul-searing pain – were the same.

In the ten years since our son breathed his last, I have experienced what many call the journey of grief. For those who don't know me, when I want to do something, and have any chance of doing that something right, I like to take in information about it. No, strike that. I *consume* any and all information I can find on the subject, attempting to fulfill an appetite so voracious that any top-of-the-line ten course meal would fail to satisfy.

To that end, when my son died, I turned to a great number of resources "out there" about grief and the grieving process. And in my hunger for knowledge, I found what I would find when hungry for food – many options, many courses, many "meals." There are many excellent resources, many well-authored books on a subject that few like to discuss.

So why write my own book about grief? My answer is two-fold:

I've taken the journey.

That's what grief is, really – a journey. This journey varies from person to person, from experience to experience. Prior to the death of our son, I twice went on two differing versions of this journey; first with my maternal grandmother, second with my paternal grandfather. Those experiences, those journeys, were vastly different from the one I am taking initiated by the death of my son. Regardless, I have and continue to travel this journey, which brings me to the second reason for writing this book.

I'd like to invite you to join me in my travels.

You, my dear reader, fall into one or more of three distinct categories:

Those Who Have Yet to Find Reason to Grieve

Perhaps you have yet to see and feel the sting of death in your life – to yet have it visit a close loved one. To be honest, I envy you. Death's sting is indeed painful as it is sharp and deep. But as the old cliché goes, there are two guaranteed things in this world: death and taxes. Without sounding too morbid, if you have any attachments at all – family, friends, loved ones – you will experience the effects of the death of a loved one, and it is my hope that this book will prepare you for the inevitable journey of grief that will follow. As it does so, I also hope that it will enable you to come alongside someone currently undertaking the treacherous but rewarding journey of grief.

Those Who Have Grieved in the Past

Or perhaps death has already come to a loved one, albeit many years ago. Maybe you barely took the first couple of steps on your personal journey of grief, or because of the difficulty of it all, avoided it altogether. Maybe you decided it was best to "get over it" and get on with your life. It is my hope for you that my personal account will inspire you to resume your journey, to return to the path, to follow it wherever it might lead, in order that your day-to-day life might benefit from doing so.

Those Who are Actively Grieving

Lastly, perhaps you have recently experienced the death of a loved one. Perhaps you are actively walking out your journey as you read this; walking (or more likely trudging) through pain, burdened by heartache and sorrow. For you, the simple act of picking this book up off the shelf felt like lifting a hundred-pound weight. For you, my hope is that you know you are not alone. I walk with you. Yes, our paths are different. And yet they are very similar. I hope that I might encourage you as we walk together, you and me – as well as the countless others alongside us.

With that, I invite you to take a step, to turn the page. I invite you to walk with me through grief. In the coming pages, I will detail my personal nine-day journey starting with having a perfectly healthy sixteen-month-old boy ending with our walking through death's doorstep and beyond. I will also share the lessons I have learned from the journey, the lessons that have certainly held truth for me, and that will do the same for you if given the chance. Ultimately, I endeavor to show you that good grief, when embraced in its fullness, will enable you to derive life from the otherwise barren wasteland that is death.

So will you walk with me? Let's begin where it all began for me:

the birth of our boy.

CHAPTER 2

A New Life

SATURDAY, APRIL 6, 2002

I'm a natural-born night owl. Have been one as long as I can remember. If allowed to waken at a natural time, I might be lucky to find one or two dried out half-eaten pieces of worm jerky; the early birds certainly would have consumed the rest during the morning hours through which I blissfully slept.

Because of this backwards nocturnal-based DNA, when I'm *not* allowed to waken at a time more comfortable for me, I can be a very grumpy night owl. On the best of typical mornings, I'm all bark, some bite, and very groggy.

But the morning of April 6, 2002, was far from a typical morning for me.

When the alarm shocked me loose from my slumber, my eyes struggling to creak open, the sun not yet making its appearance on the horizon, I awoke with a smile on my face. I knew that in a few short hours, my wife Jenna and I would, for the first time, enter a new life – a life as parents.

Jenna, having developed gestational diabetes during pregnancy, required a Caesarian section. Although not the birthing plan she originally desired, it carried with it one huge advantage: we knew when our child would be born. (Although if you asked her, she might say another huge advantage was being able to "beautify" herself by putting on make-up and the like before the big event.)

Assuming the incredibly proficient ultrasound tech from months prior was not a night owl like myself and half-asleep while doing her job, we also knew that we were about to welcome a new baby boy into the world. His name was already chosen:

Micah Anthony Martin Miller

I was excited to welcome into this world a boy – a *son*. Long since a proud amateur family historian, I longed to have a boy to carry forth our surname, despite it being a surname whose only claim to fame is having an alcoholic beverage named after it. Being our first, we also decided to give him two middle names – like his mother – honoring both of our fathers. I do not wish to imply that I think more highly of boys than I do girls (I hoped for at least one of each before our baby-making days were done). But there was something almost magical about our first child being the long hoped for son.

A son. My son. Our son.

There is something that reverberates within a man when he thinks on these words. My son would be perfect, of course – carrying only the finest genes from Jenna and me. He would be handsome. He would be intelligent. His alabaster skin would bronze in summer. He would aspire to do great things, to change the world even. He would protect any potential future sisters he might have. He would teach me valuable life lessons as I did the same for him. He would, much as I did, marry a wife that would make him a better man. He would have children of his own. And through all of this, I would cherish him, love him, and be proud of him until the day I died.

This grand adventure that would be my son's life would begin in an operating room of a hospital that saw many come before and after. As I stood in that operating room, Jenna already prepped on the table for surgery, I was eager to begin that journey.

Then, before I had time to fully comprehend what was about to happen, as the doctor began the incision that would open the door through which my son would enter the world, I beheld the first of many marvels that were to come that day. A drape divided Jenna in two. To my right, she was alert, awake, and conversed with me as if it were any other normal Saturday morning. To my left, the doctor was making incision after incision into her abdomen, skillfully and rapidly removing each barrier between himself and our Micah. When I asked her if she felt anything at all, she simply said, "Yes, a little pressure, I think... but that's it." In that moment, I was thankful for modern medicine's contributions that enabled such a birth to take place with little risk to mother or infant.

Shortly thereafter, that marvel that so occupied my mind was replaced with the one that blew it out of the water. The last barrier to extra-uterine life breeched, the doctor pulled Micah's head from the opening in Jenna's belly. Vigorously suctioning fluid from his airway, the medical team pulled his entire body upward and out. As the doctor did so, he said, "That's a good-sized baby." Apparently very worried about his body image, Micah released his first cry into this world for all to hear. I started to cry. Jenna started to cry. And our son continued to cry.

It was a veritable Miller family river of tears.

The minutes that followed whirred by in rapid succession, leaving only the faintest of blurs of memory in my mind. The nurses did what they were trained to do. The doctors did what they were trained to do. Jenna's surgery, once completed, was described as "textbook." Our son, all 9 pounds 5 ounces of him, was as perfect as we imagined.

His grand adventure, and ours, had begun.

CHAPTER 3

Dreams

*D*reams completely and utterly fascinate me. Sure, I've had the proverbial dreams where I address a crowd of people dressed in little more than my underwear. I've had dreams that were far more anxiety-riddled, however: forgetting my lines to a play or a speech while on stage; realizing I haven't studied for the big exam I'm currently seated to take; going through one phase where I consistently dreamt of being shot, all in various locations during various circumstances; there was even one dream starring an evil Bert and Ernie.

But I've had great dreams, too. I enjoyed one of my particularly favorite dreams just a short couple of years ago: in this dream, I could fly. This wasn't just a "fly around, look at the scenery" sort of dream; I actually *felt* what I imagine being able to fly would feel like. My stomach twisted and turned much like it does when riding an exhilarating roller coaster. The wind rushed past and around my ears as I changed direction. I could go where I want, when I wanted, taking off and landing with ease.

And, for some reason unknown to me, a great number of my dreams take place in what I can only surmise is some sort of spiritual epicenter for me – my paternal grandmother's house. And all of these dreams vary greatly: good dreams, weird dreams, bad dreams... Dreams with friends, strangers, and on one occasion, zombies. There have been floods at grandma's house. There have been enemy attacks. Grandma is sometimes there. Sometimes my grandfather, who has been dead some twenty years now, is there as well. In one dream, despite being nothing more than a gentle loving giant to me during his lifetime, he even choked me in that house.

Pretty sure Freud could have a field day with that one.

These sleeping dreams, the ones by which our minds repair and reorganize, are the kind that we have in common with many types of animals. It has been shown that animals dream while they sleep – cats, dogs, even rats. Many pet owners can vouch for this, watching their beloved dog or cat twitch as they chase some unseen prey over imagined (or remembered) landscapes.

Yet these are not the dreams I wish to focus on in this chapter. The dreams I would like to turn your attention to are the dreams that I contend separate us from the animals – the dreams we have while wide awake. Not the daydreams that lazily invade our brain when it should be focused on tasks such as learning, completing a task, having a conversation, or driving... but *dreams*. Intentional dreams that cause us to reach, to strive, to improve.

A friend once reminded me we aren't all dreamers, not in the "dream big life- and world-changing dreams" sense of the word. And she's right. Yet I contend that we all have dreams – some big, some small – but dreams just the same. What dreams do you have?

Do you dream of one day finding Mr. or Mrs. Right?

Do you dream of having children?

Do you dream of being the best at what you do?

Do you dream of getting out of the slums, making a better and brighter future for yourself?

Do you dream of furthering your education to get that dream job, that dream promotion, or that dream career change?

Do you dream of visiting a long-distance relative again? Of seeing your grandmother, grandfather, father, or mother one more time before they die?

Do you dream of conquering some mountain before you, some obstacle in your way? Of fighting and beating cancer?

Do you dream of working hard now so you can play hard later? Of a wealth-filled retirement?

Do you dream of a future in which your children can succeed, one that you have a hand in preparing them for?

The list of potential dreams is as exhaustive as it is inspiring. This is but one thing that separates man from animal. After all, I've never heard of a cat or dog dreaming of going to college.

It is on this basis that I'd like to offer an alternative definition of the word grief, one I had never heard of before, one that will serve as a compass by which we make our way through the treacherous journey that can be grief.

Grief is... a dream interrupted.
Grief is... a dream reclaimed.

When Micah was born, we had many dreams for him and our life together with him. In addition to the dreams we had for him, we had personal dreams we strived for. Like many couples, we dreamed of a day when we could be debt-free. We dreamed of making a better life for our small family. We had recently moved almost 300 miles from the Seattle area to Spokane, Washington, away from 98 to 99 percent of our family and friends, in order that I might pursue my newly-discovered dream of obtaining a nursing degree.

When Micah died, our dreams had to be placed on hold. *Grief is... a dream interrupted.* When death made its uninvited visit to our family, life was clicking along at its usual breakneck pace, only to come to a screeching halt. Death has a way of doing that. Things that mattered before are placed in a greater perspective, set aside for the purpose of dealing with Death's good friends – Pain, Sorrow, and Despair.

And it is in this "dealing" with pain, sorrow, and despair, taking this journey of grief, that the second part of the definition of grief is realized. Although a loved one cannot return from the dead, although your life is irrevocably changed after the death of a loved one, dreams themselves can be reclaimed.

Some dreams can be resumed, as in the case of my pursuit of a nursing degree. Some dreams change. And further still, you can find yourself dreaming new dreams. But in all of them, the memory of your loved one's life remains, in a way adding new life to reclaimed dreams. *Grief is... a dream reclaimed.*

As we take this journey together over the next several chapters, it is my hope that you will reclaim your dreams, or at the very least begin to see that they can be reclaimed at a future time. The great thing about dreams is that they inherently carry with them hope. A dream cannot be realized unless the dreamer believes – that is, has hope – that it can be brought to life. It is this hope that will become an ever-present companion on your journey of grief. It is also by this hope that we can begin to derive life from death on the journey of grief. This will be an invaluable compass, dreams and hope combined, lighting the way through what right now very likely feels like a dark and empty road.

One last note before we leave this chapter. This definition of grief is not intended to be a mantra of any kind, though if it helps, write it down and use it as such. It did not serve as a mantra for me, as it was only in retrospect that I discovered this principle. If I had known then what has been made evident to me now, perhaps I would have been better prepared for the day that forever altered our grand adventure, set us on the journey of grief, and radically changed our lives... the day of the accident.

CHAPTER 4

An Argument, a Stroll, and a Late Summer Sun

SUNDAY, AUGUST 24, 2003

*W*hat did you like to play during elementary school recess? If any of my friends needed to find me, they knew where to look: the wall ball court. Despite my childhood adoration with this game, I am firmly convinced that only children could find hitting a ball against a wall any great source of competitive fun.

While many other boys and I took turns hitting a rubber ball against a wall, many of the girls could be found doing something arguably saner: playing on the monkey bars. I never understood the appeal of monkey bars; what fun was there in swinging from rung to rung, over and over again? (Especially when compared to the utter thrill of hitting a ball against a wall, over and over again.)

Don't get me wrong; I did actually *try* the monkey bars once. Some cute girl talked me into it. She must have been really cute, because she convinced me to attempt something I thought was extremely dangerous – hanging upside down. I remember the moment when, legs wrapped around the bar at my knees, hands firmly attached to the bar in a death grip, I let go and let swing.

My world completely flipped upside down.

For a moment, watching my friend and the playground zip from rightside-up to upside-down, I thought the monkey bars might be cool after all. However, momentum didn't allow me that thought; my body swung fast enough that my legs, forgetting their only task in this new experience, slipped from the bar, causing my face to meet the rubber mat below.

I've never cared for monkey bars since.

Little did I know on Sunday, August 24, 2003, a set of figurative monkey bars waited for me. Around seven o'clock in the evening, my world would once again be completely flipped upside down.

The day started off innocently enough, masquerading as a typical Sunday for us at the time. After attending Sunday morning service at our home church, practicing our faith as we knew it then, we had errands to run. Thankfully enough, there weren't many that day; two, to be exact. One was mundane – the standard run to the grocery store to stock up on food and supplies before starting a new work week on Monday. The other, however – well, it was one that rarely if ever occurs, and one that can loosely be described as the catalyst for all that was to follow.

Jenna and I, like every other married couple on the face of the planet, have our disagreements. We can frustrate each other, not see eye-to-eye, and even get angry with one another. But one thing we never do is fight. We don't yell. We don't scream. We don't fight. If ever we did, this Sunday would have been the day for it.

This seemingly innocuous second errand involved purchasing and returning equipment for a newly obtained five gallon fish tank. This fish tank was gifted to us by Jenna's mother – something for Micah to enjoy. Jenna and I held two different viewpoints regarding this fish tank. She thought it would make a nice addition to our home, something that Micah would be thrilled by. I saw it as something that would require additional expenditures of both time and money, both of which were in short supply. Needless to say, my beautiful wife convinced me to take the family to the pet store after church in order to pick out rocks, fish, and decorations that I had neither interest in or patience for. What can I say? I've always had a thing for cute girls.

Wanting to please my wife, I purchased the necessary fish tank paraphernalia, mumbling under my breath as I did so. However, the stubborn side of me won out prior to our driving out of the parking lot. In the safety of our car, away from the prying eyes of the pet store employees, I told Jenna that we really couldn't afford the items we just purchased after all, and decided then and there that they must be returned. Yes, despite having just walked out of the store with them, and despite wanting to please my wife, as I said before, my stubborn side won out. As if this weren't enough, I didn't have the courage or desire to do it myself. I made Jenna do the "dirty work." Was I a jerk? Absolutely. Did Jenna yell or scream at me? Nope. She submitted to my woefully pitiful request, returned the items, and then rightfully proceeded to not talk to me for the duration of the ride home. An errand, turned into a disagreement, turned into frustration, anger, and friction.

We have ways of dealing with these things (on the *rare* occasions that they occur, mind you). I humbled myself, apologized for being a stubborn ass, and did my best to make amends. We ended up laying Micah down for his afternoon nap, and then played a remarkably calm game of Clue: Master Detective, discussing our options regarding the fish tank while simultaneously accusing Colonel Mustard and his peers of wrongdoings.

Given the tense interactions of earlier in the day, we decided to take a walk around our neighborhood sometime that evening shortly before seven o'clock. It is a walk we had taken numerous times before; a walk that usually contained excitement no greater than that provided by noticing a neighborhood pet or a new passer-by. Little did we know that when we walked out of our door for our walk that evening, we wouldn't walk back through it for almost an entire week.

On the last stretch of that walk, with not even five to ten minutes duration remaining, we strolled into the late summer sun. There was not a cloud to be seen. Walking on a sidewalk, against traffic, we continued through a typical suburban neighborhood. Something caught our eye. A stereotypically snobbish and self-absorbed cat sat perched on a fence of an empty house. Carefully looking both ways before crossing the street, we walked onto the empty house property, peering inside. As we resumed our walk, we talked about our dream of one day owning a home, much like the one we had just peered into. As we strolled, now so close to the next cross street, staying on the gravel shoulder walking in the direction of traffic, we were consumed with dreams of being homeowners, not apartment renters. We imagined the empty living room no longer empty, but filled with our furniture; the empty kitchen decorated just right by my lovely wife; the empty bedroom filled with Micah's crib and toys.

A minivan, containing a family very similar to ours both in family members and ages, drove into the same late summer sun. What errand summoned them from their house I do not know. What events on a typical or atypical Sunday they experienced prior to that moment I also do not know. What I do know, however, is that in that moment, shortly before seven o'clock in the evening, our lives merged; their lives were to be as radically changed as ours.

That late summer sun, blinding the driver and his wife, caused him to adjust his wife's visor. In the process of doing so, for whatever reason, his minivan drifted to the right. With a crash, a large round starburst indentation appeared as if from nowhere over his wife's field of view. Having prior experience in landscaping, the driver thought someone had thrown a large rock over a fence, landing on his windshield.

If only that had been the case.

Instead, it was Micah who caused the indentation. Finishing our walk in a child carrier strapped to my back, he and I were hit from behind, the minivan's bumper striking me squarely behind my knees. The force of the impact sent us back into the windshield, then forward some 57 feet (a little over three times the length of the minivan that hit us). Walking directly next to me, the love of my life, the mother of our child, became witness to the entire event, helpless as she watched her entire life change before her eyes. She screamed. A couple of Good Samaritans came to her assistance.

I was unaware of anything. Most of what I've written here was later pieced together from police reports, witness reports, and Jenna's own view of the accident. Micah lay completely still on the gravel. I apparently tried to sit up, utterly confused and not my normal self. Before long, a neighbor called 911, ambulances arrived, and we were whisked away separately to a local hospital. Jenna rode with our son, knowing that if he were to waken, he would need her more than I. All the while she longed to know how I was.

And how was I? I entered what I describe as "radio silence"–the period of time from the moment of impact to the hour I woke – in which I have no recollection of anything that occurred. Jenna later told me a funny story–one of very few that would happen in the days to come–that happened on this day, during a moment she was with me on the way to the trauma room. At some point after arriving at the hospital, I was lying completely naked, covered only by a sheet, on a stretcher in the hospital's Emergency Room. As the nurses tend to me, I turn to Jenna and apologetically mutter, "Honey, I'm sorry they're looking at my butt." She is quick to console me. After a brief moment of silence, I turn to the nurses and sheepishly ask, "Is it a nice one?"

Nice to know what my true priorities are when I no longer have control over my consciousness; a consciousness, by the way, that I wouldn't regain until early the next day.

CHAPTER 5

How Rude

*H*ow rude of me. I just realized I have violated one of the central tenets taught to me by my mother, my father, and every adult figure I had growing up: I have not taken the time to properly introduce myself.

Here I am prattling on about dreams, rushing headlong into Micah's story, without so much as a "hi, how do ya do?" So if you don't mind, I will briefly give you a little personal background. I hope it will give you a greater understanding of who I am, and more importantly, how "who I am" plays into my journey of grief.

In the interest of rapidly returning you to the rest of this book – the stuff that *really* matters – let me extend my hand and introduce myself.

Hello, my name is Eric and... I'm an optimist by nature. For me, the glass is always better half-full. For some, this might be irritating. I'd like to think that everyone loves an optimist, but that's just me being optimistic. Regardless, even the glass-half-fullest of us all can find optimism to be in rare supply when faced with grief. And that's okay.

Hello, my name is Eric and... I once was a paradoxically socially inept butterfly. Or an ugly duckling turned swan. Take your pick. Picture a boy both tall and slender, as gracefully athletic as a foal learning how to walk, dressed in the finest second-hand USA Today sweatshirt while refusing to wear anything other than sweatpants to cover his legs, a pair of too-big-for-his-face glasses perched atop his too-big-for-his-face nose, braced teeth, topped off with golden not-so-flowing locks molded into a behind-the-times mullet... you get the idea. And despite all of this, I was an extroverted social butterfly. I never could understand how one person could be simultaneously socially driven and inept, despite living it out on a daily basis.

This portrait of my awkward youth is significant in that I assumed it would forever prevent me from having the deeply desired family of my own that I longed for for as long as I can remember. To have my assumption proven wrong by marrying the love of my life and having our first child, only to then lose that child to death, caused a heartache compounded twice over.

Hello, my name is Eric and... I like movies. You might find a few cinematic references to death or grief sprinkled here-or-there.

Hello, my name is Eric and... I call things as they are. This has become truer since the accident. I don't consider myself to be brash or calloused; I merely find it difficult to take the time to beat around the bush after experiencing how quickly our time in this life can end. To that end, in the coming chapters, I will not pull any punches. I will describe in detail what we experienced, how I felt, and what transpired during those first few days on our journey of grief. However...

My name is Eric and... I like to make people laugh. Death, grief, and their associated topics are not ones that tend to produce much laughter. As I said before, I promise to pull no punches in the coming chapters, but I will strive to do so in a way that will not leave you in darkness greater than you experience now; you do not need somebody else's sadness added to yours. Instead, my experience will be used only to bring you to a place of hope. It is my hope that, over the coming pages, we will both cry *and* laugh together. At the very least, if you won't laugh with me, I invite you to laugh *at* me, even if it only provides you a brief respite from your current troubles.

Hello, my name is Eric and... I believe in God. I have done so for as long as I can remember. In my previously described ugly duckling youth, I recall looking at all the wonders contained within nature and finding it difficult to believe it occurred all by accident, that somehow, a Supreme Being must exist. I recognize that you might not. If that is the case, please know that a belief in God is not required to apply the principles found in this book. I don't even consider it a goal of mine to make you a believer in God. Yet, because I believe that He is a very real being – not a social construct or mental crutch – and one that takes a personal interest in His creation, I cannot separate my belief in Him from my experience on our journey of grief. And, to take this particular introduction one step further...

Hello, my name is Eric and... I believe that Jesus is God. I committed my life to Him at the age of 17, and since that time have made faith in Him paramount in my life. To clarify, my faith is not in organized religion (man's attempt to relate with God), but in relationship (God's attempt to relate with man). It is not my purpose in this book to defend His existence, let alone the veracity of the claims made about Him in the Bible. Nor is it my purpose to "Bible thump" you into taking the exact same journey through grief that I am taking. You will, however, see this belief crop up from time to time, either in specifically referenced Scripture, or simply mentioned in passing.

Thank you for taking a moment to get to know me better. My ultimate point in providing this personal background is this:

Whether or not you are an extroverted social butterfly or an introverted meek and mild lamb,

whether your glasses are perpetually half-empty or half-full,

whether you prefer a good movie or a good book,

whether you believe in God or not,

regardless of status, wealth, position, popularity, situation in life...

...we are all united by those events and experiences that transcend "us" and "our little worlds," not the least of which is the journey of grief we will all likely take at one time or another, beginning with the death of a dearly loved friend... family member... fellow human being.

Now that we are no longer strangers, please walk with me into Day Two of my grief journey. It takes place on a Monday; while most people tried to get to work that morning, I simply tried to get my brain to work.

CHAPTER 6

A Tale of Two Mornings

MONDAY, AUGUST 25, 2003

My Monday, the morning after the day of the accident, starts unlike any other that came in the twenty-plus years prior. Sometime around five o'clock in the morning, I wake up as from an ordinary deep sleep, look at the clock on the wall, foggily drink in my foreign surroundings, realize that I am certainly not in the comfort of my own room, and conclude that something unusual has happened. My brain might not have been firing on all cylinders, but enough of them were working well enough to get the job done.

The feeling was rather surreal. My senses gathered enough information to know that I was in a hospital room of some sort, but for the life of me couldn't determine how or when I got there. Before I even had a moment to remember I had a wife and child, let alone wonder where they might be, Jenna walked into the room.

As I see her, my face becomes a mixture of relief and wonderment. I ask her where we are. "Sacred Heart Medical Center," she replies. I ask her what happened. She tells me that Micah and I had been hit by a car. My face contorts into a very painful expression. I ask her how Micah is. She tells me he's okay, and the doctors think he'll be fine. As I take this new information in, she asks, "Don't you remember me telling you this before?" "Of course not," I reply. She then explains that for the last hour or so I've ridden this entire relief/shock/sadness/relief merry-go-round over and over and over again. In my eagerness to set her heart at ease, I exclaim, "But this time I'm really awake! I really understand!" Instead of breathing a sigh of relief, however, she simply replies:

"You've said that before too."

My loving wife then spoke some long forgotten comforting words to me and encouraged me to get back to sleep, likely not fully believing that everything she told me had truly sunk in. As I drifted off, returning to the concussion-induced stupor from which I had briefly woken, I recall wondering if she had any opportunity to get some sleep herself. I also recall wishing I could hold my son again, to verify that all she had said was true, but was quickly overtaken by my body's desire for whatever sleep it desperately needed.

I awoke again sometime later that morning at a far godlier hour, reassured once again by my surroundings that what I had experienced a few hours before had not been a dream. As I said before, this Monday was unlike any other, as prior to this point, I had never been hospitalized. Sure, there were numerous emergency room visits as a child on account of being a card-carrying asthmatic, as inhaler-dependent as Mikey from the movie *Goonies*. Sure, I had even broken my arm once. But never had I required a hospitalization. At least my experience was not so serious that I required a stay in the Intensive Care Unit. Instead, I had been admitted to the Neurological Unit, obviously related to the altered state of mind which led me to ask nurses about the quality of my rump the night before.

After looking up at the television and seeing a brief news snippet pertaining to our accident (which coincidentally followed two news snippets about other disasters: an overturned van in Utah carrying a lot of people, and my hapless Mariners losing a very important game to the Red Sox), I had the privilege of partaking in another "funny" moment. After having never called in sick to work in the year I had lived in Spokane, I called my boss. Fully reveling in the moment, my conversation with her went something like this...

> *"Yah, um, I think I'm going to have to call in sick today."*
> *[Really, why?]*
> *"Well, I kind of got hit by a car yesterday."*
> *[That was YOU?!]*

To this day, even after all that happened, I'm still humored by that conversation. It was a light-hearted moment that helped carry me through what I thought would be the worst of our experience over the next couple of days. It carried me through the remainder of my stay in that hospital room that day. It carried me through being discharged from one room, only to go stay with Micah in another. And it carried me most when I first laid eyes on my beautiful baby boy, lying motionless in a crib, somewhat recognizable behind his newly obtained c-collar and bruised and swollen eyes.

CHAPTER 7

The Elephant

Say I'm in a room with other people and the proverbial elephant. The number of people doesn't matter. The size of the room doesn't matter. The room's décor – you guessed it – doesn't matter. What matters is that *there is a ridiculously large pachyderm in the room!*

I understand the *idea* behind ignoring the proverbial elephant in the room. But have you been to the zoo? Have you seen an elephant? Better yet, have you *smelled* an elephant? No way Dumbo's getting intentionally overlooked.

And yet the subjects of death and grief, while experienced

by someone, somewhere, every single day, often go ignored, not discussed. Based on this fact alone, I can consider it a miracle if you have purchased this book and are still with me, reading these words right now. So why is this "grief" thing such a taboo subject for most? I propose three reasons:

1. Death and grief are uncomfortable subjects. No one wanting to appear sane starts a conversation off by eschewing typical openers such as "Looks like good weather next week" or "How 'bout them Yankees?" by instead opening with "So, how are you preparing for the death of a loved one today?"

2. Our everyday life is filled with the mundane and superficial. "How are you doing?" has become a greeting on par with "Hello," often uttered without the expectation of an answer. By their very nature, death and grief are deep subjects, prompting further topics of discussion such as belief systems, paradigms, and spirituality, all the while touching people in a deeply emotional way.

3. Talking about death and grief reminds us of our own mortality. And really, who wants to be reminded of that?

Am I encouraging more open discussion about death and grief? Absolutely – but with caution. We must take great care to not swing so far in the other direction that we obsess over it. I'd hate to see us end up like poor Sigmund from *What About Bob?* (If you have not seen this movie yet, I beg you to do so soon; the laugh per minute quotient could be very therapeutic... just wait until you finish reading this book, of course). In the beginning of the movie, the young boy Sigmund discusses his fear of death with the titular adult, Bob, as played with the comedic genius of a Bill Murray at the top of his game.

Sigmund: Bob?

Bob: Yeah?

Sigmund: Are you afraid of death?

Bob: [thinks for a moment] Yeah.

Sigmund: Me too. There's no way out of it. You're going to die. I'm going to die. It's going to happen. What difference does it make if it's tomorrow, or eighty years? Much sooner in your case. Do you know how fast time goes? I was six like yesterday.

Bob: Me too.

Sigmund: I'm going to die. You... are going... to die. What else is there to be afraid of?

Understand that although death is discussed in this book, it is not to be the *focus* of this book. Instead, it is my aim to show how life can be derived from death, how the journey of grief can be successfully navigated. Also understand that although the topic of grief can be rightfully associated with life-changing events like the loss of a job or the breakup of a relationship, our journey of grief will focus entirely on that which takes place after the death of a loved one.

So how do we prepare for the death of a loved one? How do we adequately "pack" for this journey of grief? There is but one easy answer to these questions:

Shut everyone out of your life now and forever more.

Gosh, that was easy. I suppose there's nothing more to be said. Thanks for joining us, have a nice day, don't let the door hit you on the way out...

And yet that solution could never truly work, could it? Sure, if there was no one to love, no one to bond with, no one to make an impact on your life, then there would be no one to grieve over when they died, no pain to be experienced upon their death, right?

But if we extrapolate that solution out to its very end, we would find a very dark, cold, and loveless life. Life was not meant to be lived alone. We cannot successfully navigate life, let alone the journey of grief, without the enrichment we find from befriending and loving others. It's risky though, isn't it? Love is risky. We risk loving another despite the pain that would come with that person's death.

Which brings us back to our original question: How do we adequately pack for this journey of grief? Whenever Jenna and I go on a trip, we have two very different ideas of what needs to be packed. Jenna likes to be prepared. For, say, a three day trip, she likely has six or seven outfits, multiple pairs of footwear, apparatuses for both curling and straightening hair, cosmetics, toiletries, umbrellas, sun screen – and that's just the carry-on bag. (Maybe I'm stretching the truth a bit here, but if that's you, be rest assured there's nothing wrong with that – pack away!)

I, however, am much simpler by nature. For the same trip, I might pack two complete outfits (I'll be wearing one on the day of departure, after all), some cologne, and a good book (you never know when a good book might come in handy). With this simplicity in mind, I offer you six things you might pack for your journey of grief – three things to know, and three things to do – all of which will not only serve to help prepare you for the journey, but will enrich your present-day life as well.

Three Things to Know

When faced with the death of a loved one, life takes on a whole new meaning.

Four months after the accident, one week before Christmas, our car was one of two lucky cars selected to be broken into. At the time, our car was somewhat akin to a second storage for us (although I embrace simplicity, maintaining a clean environment has never been one of those simplicities). Many of our belongings, including our car stereo and over 60 CDs, were taken. Such an event would normally have sent me into fits of rage. Being hit by a van and watching my son die brought a new perspective to my life, however. Allow this "new perspective" to permeate every area of your life now, *before* the death of a loved one.

Understand that bad things can and do happen to good people.

You need not look any further than the daily news to confirm this – a teacher improving the lives of impoverished children goes missing; a Good Samaritan is murdered by the hitchhiker he picked up; average citizens and children being randomly selected for murder – it is a sad but unfortunate truth.

Nor is this truth limited to modern times. The biblical account of Job, believed by many scholars to have been the oldest book of the Bible, gives the quintessential example of a good man who suffers. In it, Job is described as a man that was "blameless and upright, one who feared God and turned away from evil." If you read the book of Job, you find that this "upright" man loses almost everything he has – his wealth, his ten children, and his health. If a man so biblically described as blameless and upright can lose so much, what hope is there for you and me?

Yet it is my hope that the takeaway from knowing this truth is this: you are not alone in your suffering. Good people do not receive a "get out of grief free" card. Death and grief are universal. In that respect, I and many others are here for you.

Death is bad; grief is good.

When the journey of grief is embraced and embarked upon, it is good. Dictionaries describe grief as "deep mental anguish," "annoyance," "frustration," "trouble," "difficulty," "affliction," "sorrow," "suffering," and "deep and poignant distress." Taking the journey of grief myself, however, I posit this alternate definition: Grief is the process by which we learn how to *live life* after the death of someone we love. By walking grief's path, we can transform death into life.

Three Things to Do

Draw close to loved ones before tragedy strikes.

There are two sides to this coin. As proven by our accident and countless others before it, tragedy can strike at any time.

However, there is also no guarantee that tragedy will visit your loved one. Either way, do me a favor, and *spend time with your loved ones while you still can.* Hug your kids tighter before they go to sleep. Give your spouse a deep, passionate kiss before they leave for work. Have that coffee with your mother, your father, your friend. In the grand scheme of humanity's history on this planet, you and your loved one's 50-, 60-, even 90- or 100-plus years of life are but a breath. Don't take another day or hour for granted.

Draw close to God before tragedy strikes.

I've said it before, and I'll likely say it again: God is not a crutch created by man upon which to lean during difficult times. He's real. He walks with me on my journey, and He'll do the same for you if you allow. Speaking of, I'd like to get a little more specific if you don't mind...

Memorize Scripture.

Again, it is not my purpose to "Bible thump" you into taking the same journey I take. But know that there is a comfort to be found in the pages of the Bible that can't be found in books like this (despite my best intentions to the contrary). Find Scripture that means something to you, something that resonates, comforts, or just plain uplifts. Then memorize it. Please trust me – it will come in *very* handy when you find yourself in the midst of darkness you have never known.

And for those that have the desire but think they lack the ability, I offer you this. Can you recall doing something in the

last year, month, or even week that you knew you weren't supposed to do but did anyway? Perhaps even beat yourself up
over it? We human beings with a conscience are very good at
keeping track of the things we do wrong. I can even tell you
the shameful things I did years ago. Now if we take half the
energy we use to remember our record of wrongdoings and
instead apply it to memorizing Scripture, how much could we
memorize? It's a sobering thought – for me, at least.

With all this talk of drawing close to God and memorizing Scripture, I'm sure you'd think I was absolutely
prepared for what was to come with our son Micah. I'm
sure you think that my faith in God was pumping along at
its fullest.

Well, unfortunately, that wasn't the case.

CHAPTER 8

Everything's Gonna Be A-Ok

TUESDAY, AUGUST 26, 2003

F aith in doctors was, for the time being, still greater than faith in God.

Whoa! What a shocking, scandalous, and practically sacrilegious thing for a Bible-believing Christian to say! Let me explain.

On Tuesday, two days after the accident, hope in the "natural" still existed. Micah's prognosis from the beginning was good. Although he had not regained consciousness at any time, doctors were sure he would recover on his own by Wednesday morning.

We believed them. How couldn't we? Despite the fact that he hadn't woken since the accident, our son looked very much like a somewhat bruised but normal boy, save for being in a long, accident-induced sleep.

Please don't misunderstand me – Jenna and I prayed that God would indeed heal Micah and bring him around. Having been an integral part of our life, our faith hadn't wavered in any way, shape, or form. But when things look good in the natural – when circumstances are going your way – it's easy not to lean on God so heavily.

That's the place I found myself on Tuesday. Well, there, as well as "Loopyland" – not *entirely* with it, as I had only been released from my hospital room the evening before. The effects of the mild concussion I experienced still hadn't completely worn off. Yet Jenna was glad to have however much of me "back" as possible. She'd had to endure the first day of this (what we not-so-lovingly later referred to as) "Hell Week" by herself. She'd had to deal with seeing and hearing the entire accident, with not being able to be with both Micah and me while we were separated in different areas of the hospital, with making decisions while attempting to keep herself together, all without the loving support of her husband. She'd sought council with the hospital chaplain, trying to calm a storm of internal turmoil that simply didn't want to be tamed. She'd tried to comprehend every life-changing minute that transpired over the previous couple of days. But now, finally, she could deal with it all with the help of "half" of her husband – Loopyland Miller.

So with little changes in Micah's status, and with little desire to do anything else or be anywhere else, Tuesday became a day of waiting. Waiting for Micah to "wake up." Waiting for the little boy we loved with all of our hearts to come back. Waiting for the neck brace to come off. Waiting for his oh-so-bruised and puffy eyelids to return to normal. Waiting...

Family and friends began to arrive, visiting from around town and from the "Westside" – the Seattle area – our all-too-recently abandoned hometown. Little did we know what impact they would have in the days to come, when the "natural improvement" of our son was instead replaced with something far worse....

CHAPTER 9

Everybody Needs Somebody

In the late 1980s, there was only one girl for me: Rae'Ann. She was the total package; she had brains, beauty, and an "it" factor that escaped description. If there was a girl in all the earth that I could be stranded with on a desert island, she was my first and only choice. The only problem?

We were in the fifth grade.

And there was no way to tell if she felt the same way.

So how does any self-respecting, socially awkward, behind-the-times kid find out if the feeling was mutual? He enlists the help of his third-grade sister.

It took a little convincing, but my sister graciously agreed to help her lovelorn brother. I'm pretty sure it was my fool-proof plan that reeled her in. The plan went a little something like this: my sister, already acquainted with Rae'Ann, would call her and make small talk. After a couple of minutes discussing the weather, school, or whatever else came to her third-grade mind, she would ease into a topic often discussed amongst girls: who does Rae'Ann like? Does she think of Eric as more than a friend?

Never one to handle suspense well, I told my sister that I would listen in on another phone upstairs. I reassured her that I would remain silent, telephone muted, so as to not rouse any suspicion from the subject of our phone call.

It was a great idea. Until it wasn't.

After what felt like an eternity, when my sister finally dropped the loaded questions, nine-plus months pregnant with anticipation, I held my breath as Rae'Ann gave her response:

I like your brother... only as a friend.

As my fifth grade heart came crashing down to earth from the heavens in which it had hovered only moments before, I blurted into the phone, "Thanks a lot, Rae'Ann!"

To this day, now decades later, I can still hear my third-grade sister fumbling awkwardly after I slammed down my phone, attempting to reassure Rae'Ann that she had no idea I was listening in.

I still consider my sister a saint for helping me through such an awkward situation so many years ago. I equally consider saints the numerous friends and family members that stepped up to help Jenna and me through the far more devastating time immediately following the accident.

In this chapter, I would like to speak directly to those who might know someone taking a journey of grief. How can you help them? What do you say? How do you come alongside people as they drag their feet, step by step, on their journey of grief?

Before I venture into a few pointers, know this: the very fact that you *want* to help someone will carry you far. Having been on the receiving end of that help, it is easy to detect the *heart* of the person offering assistance; that in and of itself goes a long way in providing help and healing for the grieving person. With that in mind, I offer these pointers for those of you who wish to comfort a person who is grieving:

First, and most importantly, having been through the fire is not a prerequisite for helping someone else through the fire.

At the time of the accident, we were close friends with about nine other couples, all of which had children of varying ages. Not one of them had ever experienced the death of their own child. Yet, to this day, despite having all moved away to the four corners of our country, they remain near and dear to our hearts. When we needed them most, they stuck with us, prayed for us, loved us, and were there for us, all despite never having personally experienced what we went through.

Ask God for wisdom.

No matter how well you know your grieving friend, God knows them better. Pray. Ask Him for guidance. Then listen. You might be surprised what you hear.

Be quick to forgive and understand.

When a person is grieving, their personality might change; they might say something out of character, or might be outright rude. Forgive them, understand them, and work with them. A couple of months after the accident, my father-in-law Dan told me, "Eric, it's good to see you making jokes again." He allowed me the time and space to deal with what was necessary before I was able to start returning to my "old self."

Use your words carefully.

Again, emotions run high for those on the journey of grief. Something you say, although intended for good, may be perceived as being hurtful. You don't have to walk on eggshells by any means. Just think before you speak. If what you intended for good is perceived as being hurtful, exercise the previous pointer – be quick to forgive and understand. And while we're on the topic of words...

Understand it's okay to not say anything.

I'm not implying that this is preferable to speaking, only that your mere presence and your listening ear can be all that the grieving friend requires. Jenna, for example, didn't necessarily need words of encouragement. Instead, what she wanted most was for loved ones to listen to her talk about her baby, about her Micah. Ultimately, when in doubt, refer to the first pointer – ask God for wisdom.

Finally, pray for your grieving friend.

During Hell Week, Jenna and I together faced the most difficult decisions I imagine any couple could possibly face. Yet, looking back on that week, we realized that it was surprisingly easy to make those decisions. We didn't notice it in the midst of the fire, but it was very evident once all was said and done. We were in agreement during that entire week. Difficult decisions, although never easy, were easier than they should have been. We know beyond a shadow of a doubt that the only reason why this was so was because of the prayer of everyone who supported us during that time. There were many people we met after the fact that knew of us and our tragedy, who didn't know us personally, who prayed for us during that week without knowing specifically what to pray for. God knew what we needed though.

Ironically enough, it was during Hell Week that I most tangibly felt the effects of the prayers of others. I had never felt it so tangibly before or since. It was this prayer that would carry us through our darkest moments – moments that began in earnest on a Wednesday morning that served as the tipping point in our journey of grief.

CHAPTER 10

New News

WEDNESDAY, AUGUST 27, 2003

*A*s was later explained to me, shortly after things had settled down the first day after the accident, Jenna was given a good prognosis for Micah. So good, in fact, that his doctors and medical team believed he would begin to "come to" sometime Wednesday morning. This news was not "false hope" news – the nurses and doctors believed it. One particular Pediatric Intensive Care Unit (PICU) nurse worked his last shift prior to going on a couple-week vacation the night

Micah was brought in. When he returned from his vacation, he was shocked and devastated to hear about how Micah's hospital stay ended up playing out. He later resigned from his position, not because of Micah specifically, but because of "all the patients like him." The EMTs and medics that came to Micah's aid were equally as shocked by what eventually happened.

Needless to say, sleep was fairly easy to come by the previous night. We went to sleep that night with great hope that Wednesday would bring the long awaited beginning to the recovery we sought. It actually ended up being the last night of "good" sleep we would have for quite some time.

Jenna, as always, woke up before me. I am unsure of everything she did that morning prior to waking me, but when she did, the look on her face told me all I would need to know for that day. The morning had not brought the beginning of recovery, but instead the beginning of heartache and death.

Doctors explained to us that at the scene of the accident Micah had more than likely stopped breathing for an indeterminate period of time. This moment, regardless of brevity, triggered brain cell death. Oddly enough, when injured brain cells begin to die, they trigger swelling in the brain. Increased brain swelling leads to increased pressure, or more specifically, ICP (intracranial pressure).

God, in His infinite wisdom, prepared us for this moment. Approximately one month before our accident, we walked through a similar tragedy with a fellow family from our previous Seattle-area church. A member of this family experienced a head-injury trauma while vacationing in Eastern Washington, and as a result had to be flown to Sacred Heart Medical Center. During that time we visited them repeatedly, praying and standing in faith for a miraculous outcome. Over the course of the time we spent with them and their situation, we learned all about ICPs, brain trauma, and what could be expected from head injury. Please don't misunderstand me – I do not imply that God *caused* this family's tragedy so that my family would benefit one month later. He simply allowed us to be a part of what that family walked through, I believe, to better prepare us for our own personal hell that was to come.

Due to Micah's increasing ICPs, it was recommended that a "bolt" be placed in his head. This "bolt" is a very sensitive device that measures a patient's ICP – intracranial pressure. A normal ICP (measured in mmHg, or millimeters of mercury), depending on your source, is less than 20; ideally it should range between 0 and 12. What we knew at that time was that a single digit ICP measurement would be desirable. Obviously, the lower the intracranial pressure, the better the prognosis Micah would receive. Due to Micah's increased ICPs, he already had to be intubated and placed on a ventilator. He couldn't breathe on his own – more bad news for our boy.

I want to be very careful about what I share next, for reasons that will be evident. We consented to the bolt surgery. Wasting no time, Micah was whisked away to the operating room. We anxiously awaited news about how surgery went, and more specifically, what his ICP number was. I never have liked hanging hope on numbers – they are but tools that medical professionals use. After all, God is bigger than numbers. We know that now, and we knew that then. But any sort of hope we could find would be as welcome as a refreshing glass of water to a desert-weary soul. Before long, we learned the surgery was successful. Micah's ICP? 9 mmHg. A single digit... praise God! Here was a tiny glimmer of hope in a day that long lost the hope it was supposed to contain.

Sometime thereafter, we were approached by another medical professional (whether a doctor or nurse, I do not recall). They took us aside and gingerly explained that there had been an error. The bolt served a dual function; not only did it measure Micah's ICPs, it served as a drain as well. When necessary, the drain could be used to help relieve pressure inside Micah's head by collecting excess cerebrospinal fluid into a reservoir bag. Again, this bolt measures the pressure of what it is directed to measure – either the pressure inside the patient's cranium, or, as was actually the case when Micah first returned from surgery, the pressure inside the reservoir bag. After someone realized the error and corrected it, Micah's true ICP was known–52 mmHg. Definitely not good.

Humans make mistakes. Understand one thing – this one didn't cost Micah his life. At 52 mmHg, Micah's pressures were so great that little could be done at that point short of a miracle. We held no ill-will toward our caregivers then, and still don't today. We received, bar-none, the absolute best care when it came to Micah. I debated even sharing this detail – it's one that only family and friends present with us that day knew about prior to making it known here. When we learned about the error, thereby revealing Micah's true ICP measurement, we were disheartened by the new number, but not surprised. The experience we had with the other family one month prior told us to expect as much. We thanked the medical professional for being open and honest with us. These things happen, after all. I can only imagine how the person who made the mistake felt.

From that point forward, the rest of Wednesday brought more of the same, yet different: more waiting. Only this time, instead of waiting for the improvement the doctors thought would come naturally, we waited to see if God would work a miracle. Though we walked out our faith to some degree prior to this moment, we suddenly received an all new perspective on what it means to walk by faith. Now that things in the natural didn't look so hot, we leaned on Christ more than ever before in our lives.

Prior to Wednesday, He was our hope. After Wednesday, He was our *only* hope.

CHAPTER 11

...a Dream Interrupted

EMBRACING GRIEF

For being such a pale-n-pasty nerdy non-athlete in my childhood, I sure did run a lot.

In junior high, my least favorite of all childhood years, there were three kids who were seemingly put on this earth for the sole purpose of tormenting me. Two years my senior, they would mock me in the cafeteria. They would make snide remarks passing in the halls. If I rode the bus home, there they would be, picking on me and other kids like me.

Not only were they amazingly cruel, but one of them had an uncanny sixth sense honed in to the whereabouts of nerds everywhere, and at times, me in particular. On days that I decided it was better for my emotional health to walk home instead of riding the bus, this particular kid knew it, anticipated it, and followed me. He'd walk a distance behind me, calling me names, verbally taunting me with as much sophistication as a junior high boy could muster. I could only take this for so long before I would run, hoping that he wouldn't have the energy to match.

I was always wrong.

This kid, every day empowered either by a hearty nutritious breakfast or the exhilaration of a nerd hunt, paced me step-for-step. I was fortunate enough that he never had a taste for combat, yet his words and taunting hurt enough. I suppose I could be thankful, however. After all, I owe whatever physical prowess I had in those days to trying to outrun this bully.

My running adventures weren't always so dramatically gloomy; looking back, I can actually laugh at a couple of the situations in which I was inspired to run.

One such example took place after a friend and I found a secret hideout in the midst of some trees outside my apartment complex. This hideout had everything a kid could want: a broken down carcass of a couch (comfortable cushions intact), an old barbeque in which anything you want could be set ablaze, and best of all, a nappy old rug upon which guests could sit.

Come to find out, we weren't the first kids to discover the hideout. Shortly after making the discovery, my friend and I were chased from the area by unseen assailants, rocks whizzing by our ears as our legs propelled us forward like gazelles from a lion. We eventually outran our attackers (*thanks for the running tips, junior high bully*), and found refuge in the apartment complex laundromat.

On yet another occasion – my favorite of them all – a different friend and I outran a gaggle of girls while dressed in faux beards, headdresses, and togas. Although I can't recount the lengthy story here, just know that it involved a series of prank calls, my friend's ex-girlfriend, and a couple of hormonally-inspired boys looking to have some wholesome fun. (For more details about this story, please read The Limited Adventures of Jamaal and Alfredo, found on our website fivearrowbooks.com.)

Although I successfully outran both the hideout attackers and the gaggle of beautiful girls, I never did outrun that junior high bully.

In the same way, you can never outrun grief.

As I turn my attention to those of you reading this book that are actively walking out your journey of grief, those of you who have recently experienced the death of a loved one, I make this point first because it is the most important of this entire chapter. It is so important that I will say it again:

You can never outrun grief.

When I was younger, a pastor once told me, "Eric, you can run from Jesus as far and as long as you like – 10 paces, 100 paces, or even 1000 paces – but you will only ever have to take one step back. He will be there, waiting for you. You can't outrun God."

Grief is strikingly similar. When a loved one dies, and pain of a greater intensity than you have ever known before saturates every fiber of your being, you have two choices. You can embrace the pain, embrace the grief, or you can run and hide.

Please don't try to run – physically, emotionally or chemically. Don't hide your pain behind busyness, alcohol, isolation, drugs, or any other equally destructive habit. You may try to do so, and with some success, but I can promise you this: your pain, your grief, they will follow you and wait for you to emerge. They will be there the moment you stop running. And they will likely find you far less capable of dealing with them than if you had embraced them in the beginning.

So wherever you are right now in your journey of grief – be it your first step or your one-hundredth – I ask you to embrace it now if you haven't done so already.

How do you embrace grief? How do you begin to deal with the intrusion of pain and hurt?

Understand that grief is a process, not a one-time event.

The bad news first: you will have shades of grief your entire life. Don't expect to ever "get over it." Not in one month, six months, or even years. Grief is the process by which we learn to live life without the presence of a loved one who inhabited it before. Life is never "normal" again.

The good news: though it may never be normal, it can get close. There can exist for you a new normal. The anguish you feel right now will not, like grief, always be there. The pain and anguish, though severe at first, will eventually lessen and dissipate, freeing you to go about the process by which normal "non-grieving" people live daily life.

When speaking to others, I liken this process to a series of waves. At first, the moments of pain and hurt are very pronounced and drawn out, with brief moments where you find yourself feeling somewhat "okay." Then, as the hours turn to days, and as the days turn to weeks, those waves change. The painful times, while still very much present and very much painful, are shorter in duration. Feeling "somewhat okay" lasts longer.

In the hours, weeks and months after the accident, I couldn't talk about Micah without becoming a sniveling, blubbering, slobbery, snot-faced mess. Jenna and I have a term for it: Ugly Face Cry. You know it – the moment when the crying becomes so intense that your face transforms from being merely disturbed, distorting into a living Picasso painting, messed up almost completely beyond recognition.

I am now ten years removed from the moment in time when my waves began, and I can say to you that I still cry. I still get emotional. But those times occur vastly less often than before. I'd say that nine times out of ten I can tell complete strangers about the accident without welling up with tears. And Ugly Face Cry still comes around, but now usually only about once per year. On that note...

Express your grief. Don't bottle everything inside.

My oldest daughter, when she was in Kindergarten, desperately wanted a cat. Not having any pets of our own at the time (save for three completely dull fish), I eventually relented when friends of ours told us a cat showed up on their door-step. After unsuccessfully searching for the kitty's rightful owners, they wanted to give the cat to us.

I brought the cat home on a Sunday. After three days of in-tense bonding with our children, the cat died on the operating table while getting spayed.

Needless to say, my kids were devastated, the Kindergart-ner taking it the hardest.

This same daughter has easily established herself as the art-ist of our family. I realize that all parents think their children are prodigies, but this girl could, at the age of five, draw better than I can right now. Unbeknownst to us, the morning after the kitty's death, she drew a four-panel story called "Dead Kitten." In it, she shows the kitten getting progressively sicker as she gets progressively sadder. The picture is included in the appendix to this book (page 163).

My daughter, wise beyond her years, expressed her grief the best way she knew how, using the gifts she has been given.

I encourage you to do the same. Find healthy outlets to express your grief, in ways both common with all (crying, shouting, seeking counseling), and in ways that are unique to your personality and talents. That is, in all reality, part of the reason why this book exists for you to read. I may be unable to draw even the simplest of stick figures, but I can write (or at least I hope I can; I suppose you can be the judge of that).

And if I may be a little more specific regarding this point:

It's okay to cry.

I'm talking to anyone who views crying as a form of weakness. I'm especially talking to you, men.

It doesn't matter how you were raised or what you've been taught – tears are the body's way of cleansing itself. This applies to all of us, of course, but I'd like to speak candidly to the men for a moment. Many times we, as men, say, "I must be strong for my family, my wife, etc." Let me tell you:

You can still be strong for others while you bawl your head off. Trust me, I've been there, and still go there from time to time.

Lastly (and this might seem a bit nitpicky):

Use and embrace the word "death."

Although true, I do not tell others that Micah "went on to a better place."

He didn't kick the bucket.

He didn't pass away.

He's not a set of car keys or a remote control; we didn't lose him.

He *died*.

There is finality to the word death that is not inherent in other phrases that we often use in its place. Other terms tend to soften the blow, to make it more palatable on the tongue.

I argue that using the word "death" itself makes it easier to embrace, enabling you to come to terms with what has actually happened, and subsequently furthering you on your continuing journey of grief.

Like I said, this point is admittedly somewhat persnickety. Using the word "death" is not a magic key to processing your grief. If you can't say it right now, that is more than understandable. We had many friends and family who could not bring themselves to say the word.

I only ask that you consider doing so in the future. I believe you will find it to be very liberating.

As Wednesday of our Hell Week gave way to Thursday, Micah was, in our minds and hearts, far from death. We continued to pray. We anxiously awaited news of our son's improvement.

Whatever things we might have received that day, news was not one of them.

CHAPTER 12

No News

THURSDAY, AUGUST 28, 2003

Wednesday night – the first of what would be many sleepless nights. It almost can go without mention, can't it? And although tossing and turning were about to become a regular exercise in my life, the first night sticks out to me, still after all these years. A sample of thoughts running through my mind:

This is the end of our "normal life" as we know it, isn't it? Where do we go from here?

What happens if I fall asleep and I miss something? What if he dies?

What if... If only... Why him... Why us... Why?

It's a wondrous thing, really. Your body is so fatigued by the crying, the questioning, the decision-making... yet it won't shut down. Mamma and Pappa Bear's cub is sick, and they want to make him better. But how? You realize that all is being done in the natural for your child – your first born – your *only* child. Yet there is nothing you can do personally to make your child better – nothing. You're absolutely, unequivocally powerless. You are void of any ability to give him a medicine that will make this all go away; unable to kiss his boo-boo in hopes of restoring health and happiness. How does a father rest in comfort knowing his only child is possibly dying in the bed next to him?

But still we had faith – and what a faith. God is a worker of miracles. We've read about miracles in the Bible. We've read about miracles in the recent past. We've even heard of miracles happening in the present. God isn't absent. His ability to work these miracles hasn't changed. And for these reasons we hope. We pray. We plead. We stand in faith, knowing that the benevolent God who has worked millions and billions of miracles can do so in our situation. He sees Micah lying on the bed. He sees our hearts – battered, broken, bleeding, but standing strong. He sees our friends and family – many of whom traveled from across state or from other states at a moment's notice – praying on our behalf. He's not deaf. He's not blind. He's God. And He now has every last ounce of control.

Faith empowers. Faith gives hope where none should exist. We woke up that Thursday morning tired beyond belief, but strengthened by the fact that all hope was not lost. Micah, at least in body, was still alive. God could still work His miracle.

Since the advent of digital cameras (and even a little while before – anyone remember the 110?), I have been what some would consider a neurotic photographer. This was only compounded with the birth of Micah. When he smiled, I took a picture. When he crawled, I took a picture. When he ate, I took a picture. When someone visited us, I took a picture of them – with Micah. I'm actually surprised I didn't take a picture of his first pee or his first poo.

Yet I look back at pictures from that day (yep – I was a neurotic picture taker even in the midst of tragedy), and all I find are three pictures. All of them are of a beautiful dog named Mowglee, a service dog that ministers to families and kids in need. That's it. No pictures of Micah. No pictures of friends. No pictures of family. Just Mowglee. Plenty of pictures of all else in the days before and after, but not on Thursday. Why? I believe it was because my mind, heart, focus, and attention were not on the current circumstances – they were directed toward God. It might have also been due to the fact that I was quite tired and didn't feel like taking pictures. But I think I'll stick to the super-spiritual reason... it sounds more sophisticated.

"Our" scripture verse – the one that adorned a handwritten poster outside Micah's room – was Philippians 4:8. It reads,

"Finally, brothers, whatever is true, whatever is honorable, whatever is just, whatever is pure, whatever is lovely, whatever is commendable, if there is any excellence, if there is anything worthy of praise, think about these things."

It might have been out of our hands entirely, but I could find no better ones to hold our situation than the Lord's.

That's how Thursday continued and ended – with no news. Nothing better, nothing worse. In our case, "no news" certainly was "good news." It freed us up to stand in faith. It freed us up to drink in the encouragement of those around us. It freed us up to have hope. And when you have hope, my friend – the kind of hope that keeps a bonfire burning deep within where every circumstance and every fiber of your being is screaming at you, demanding that you give up – with that kind of hope, what can stand in your way?

Absolutely nothing.

And that was fine by me. My appetite had already started waning; another lousy night's rest waited... but what did I care? Our faith was strong; our hope was stronger. Let tomorrow's worries come tomorrow.

And boy did they.

CHAPTER 13

Forgiveness

*T*ime: the late 1980s. Place: just outside of my good friend's neighborhood.

There I stood – adrenaline coursing through every fiber of my being, wanting to lift me high as a kite or cause me to burst forth like a cheetah. Yet I remained motionless, trapped by the millstone buried deep within my stomach. An odd mixture of regret, shame, and humility washed over me in that spot. I feebly cried out, "I'm sorry... Call you tomorrow?" as if that would come close to rectifying the situation, or at the very least relieving me of my guilt...

One of my best friends at that time was briskly walking away from me, barely within shouting distance, likely not for the purpose of getting closer to his home but to get further from me. The pain was overwhelming; in a few moments I would cry for the duration of my own walk home, betrayal and dishonor walking before me, as if to herald my coming to all who could and would hear.

My crime, at least in practicality, was minor. I intended to borrow two video games from my friend. Not steal them, mind you – just borrow. Keep in mind that I loved this friend and his entire family very dearly; they were always so kind to me, making me feel like I *was* a member of their family. One small problem: I didn't let my friend in on my plan, let alone ask him for his permission. I knew it would be successful, too. This plan, after all, would be a repeat of a plan I just success-fully completed. I already borrowed a handful of NES car-tridges – borrowed them all the way to a city 300 miles east while on my summer vacation. When I returned from vaca-tion, I had ingeniously hid them in my oversized winter coat (that I wore on a late summer day), and then feigned as if I "discovered" them in the crack of my friend's couch upon my first post-vacation visit to his house.

It is not far from the truth to say that I most certainly would have failed a life of crime if I chose to attempt one.

So on this very same visit, the one during which I made my "discovery," I repeated the plan. In a brief moment, when my friend and his family members left me alone with his small treasure trove of games, I stealthily selected another couple of titles and placed them in a worn duffel bag I brought with me.

Surely they would be so relieved that I "found" their previously-missing games, the glow of my discovery so bright, that they wouldn't notice any other games missing...

The problem with viewing my crime as one being "minor" in designation is the glaring omission of what was at the heart of this plan: a betrayal of the trust of a close friend. That and the selfish nature of the transgression itself. Placing my desires before anything else, especially the value of friendship, nearly cost me that friendship.

That lesson still hadn't made itself known to me the moment he came running after me, having not even made it more than a couple dozen paces from his house. The plan's success at that point, despite being in great jeopardy, was not dead; not in my mind, anyway. [Again, a life of crime I most obviously wasn't made for.] Even when he curtly asked to see what was in my bag, the lesson wasn't made apparent. The lesson had only sunk in when, discovering what he knew to be in my bag, he flashed me that *look*. One look from a face on which I had only ever seen smiling and laughter up to that point. The look that altogether and all-at-once said, "how... could... you..." The look that conveyed what Shakespeare penned as the dying words of the betrayed and assassinated Julius Caesar: "et tu, Brute?"

It was that look that would stay in my mind as I stood there, burning in my subconscious as the rest of me remained frozen. That look... that *lesson*... It would remain with me for the rest of my days, guiding future decisions, keeping me from similar fates, and likely only adding to my further disdain to live any sort of life of crime.

How many times have you needed forgiveness in your life? Want to know how many times I've needed it? So do I. I know they are too innumerable for me to count.

Yet I've been forgiven. I was forgiven by the friend mentioned in the account above. I've been forgiven by my wife... my mother... my father... my sisters... my brother... my friends... my coworkers... my Savior.

So I ask again: how many times have you needed forgiveness? How many times have you been forgiven? I imagine the answer is as innumerable as mine.

If not for that very reason alone, I beg of you to readily extend forgiveness to others as you take your journey of grief. You will find the opportunities to forgive astoundingly plentiful. Who do you need to forgive? The short answer is "everyone." But here are a few specific examples.

You need to forgive people who say stupid things.

I have known a great number of people who say stupid things, the chief of which I find in the mirror on a daily basis. As I mentioned in Chapter 8, "Everybody Needs Somebody," people can and will say things that can be taken in entirely the wrong way. One of my personal examples of this is when people told us, "God must have needed Micah in heaven." This was often spoken with great sincerity. Yet the immediate response that came to my mind was *God is God! He doesn't need anyone! He certainly didn't kill my son, let alone do so on account of being short one beautiful little boy in heaven.*

That may sound calloused, for which I am very sorry, but those are the kind of responses that form rapidly in a hurting and grieving mind. Yet I forgave people that said such things, not because they needed forgiveness, but because I needed to extend forgiveness for my own well-being.

Another personal example, one in which the person *did* need to be forgiven, is one that although hopefully uncommon, might be similar to an experience you have had on your own journey.

Within the first week after Micah's death and burial, Jenna went back to our Seattle-area home church to visit. A prominent member of the church, one that we knew quite well from my days employed there as a children's pastor, was standing by Jenna after service. This person was one of the few that we had not heard from during our entire ordeal.

This person turned to her, unprovoked and unprompted, and asked her, "You know why your son died, don't you?" She shook her head. They continued, "It's because you left the church in bitterness and left a door open for Satan to kill your son." I was here in Spokane attending school and going to work during Jenna's visit back "home." When Jenna called me that night and relayed what was said, I simply could not believe it. Worse than that, Jenna had to deal with what I perceived to be this person's stupidity on her own.

Yet as we reflected on the incident, it seemed as though God was asking us, "What are you going to do about it, Eric and Jenna? The appropriateness of what that person said to you is not what is at stake here. What I want from you is to know how you are going to handle it."

We understood then that the person who said these things to Jenna truly could not understand that bad things can and do happen to good people, thereby causing them to frame our tragedy within a context they could comprehend. Although it took every fiber of our beings and every last ounce of prayer, we mutually decided to extend forgiveness. The result? An eventually restored relationship with the individual, and more importantly, our freedom to continue forward in our journey of grief.

While we're on the subject, there is one more thing I would like to file under "Stupid Things People Say." And although I did find people saying this to us, I recall also saying it to others before experiencing the death of my son.

People will sometimes say, "At least your son died young. It would have been more difficult if he lived longer." Other people say the opposite: "That must be so difficult for you; if only he had lived a full life and died as an old man!"

I have come to discover that we human beings like to quantify all things – even experiences as personal as grief. A scene from *The Lord of the Rings: The Two Towers* comes to mind. King Theoden, standing outside the tomb of his own son, powerfully utters, "No parent should have to bury their child," which although moved me to impersonal tears in the theater prior to Micah's death, reduced me to Ugly Face Cry when I watched it at home after his death.

But is my loss truly that much greater than someone whose grandparent just died? What about a child who loses a parent? Is my loss less than that of a parent whose child was murdered? Is it greater than that of a mother-to-be who experiences a tragic loss through miscarriage simply based on the fact that my child lived longer?

Is any one person's grief greater than any other's? My answer: definitely not! Ask any person whose loved one has died, "How much does that hurt?" Their answer, almost every time:

A helluva lot.

You need to forgive the person or people responsible for your loved one's death.

I recognize this doesn't apply to everyone. But to those for whom it does, I again beseech you to extend that forgiveness, regardless of how difficult the task might seem.

Again we can see the need to quantify. Let me ask you this:

Who needs more forgiveness: the person who willfully murdered your loved one, or the person who *accidentally* ended your loved one's life?

The answer:

They both do.

Why? Because the forgiveness is not for the benefit of the other person. The forgiveness is for your personal benefit. The alternative is to hold on to the bitterness and anger you feel toward that person, which ultimately doesn't hurt them at all. The only person harmed by unforgiveness and bitterness is you.

I've often been asked, "What about the people who hit you? How do you forgive them?" To which I reply, "How can we not?" There are three good reasons why I chose to forgive them:

1. It is easy for me to imagine a reversal of our roles. If it were I who hit and killed their child, how much guilt and remorse would I experience?

2. What benefit would I gain from holding on to hatred, malice and unforgiveness toward them? How would that help me raise any other children we might have?

3. Most importantly, I want to be a witness for Jesus to these people. He has forgiven me of so much, how can I not do the same for them? What better opportunity is there to extend forgiveness, to preach the forgiveness of Christ to an individual?

Lastly, you need to forgive yourself.

Disturbia (2007), a movie often compared to Alfred Hitch-cock's 1954 movie *Rear Window,* tells the tale of a teen under house arrest who believes his neighbor is a serial killer. As disturbing of a premise as that is, it was the beginning of this movie that burrowed its way beneath my skin.

In one of the opening scenes, the teenager, Kale, drives a vehicle in which his father is a passenger. Through one of cinema's most disturbing vehicular accidents, Kale's father is violently killed, entirely due to Kale's poor driving.

Recognizing the scene was not real, I still asked myself the question, "How does someone like Kale recover from that?"

There is no shortage of questions pertaining to my own accident.

"Why wasn't I walking on the other side of the road, against traffic, where there was a sidewalk?"

"Why didn't I hear the van approaching?"

"Why did Micah have to be the one to take the brunt of the impact? Why not me?"

What questions might you find yourself asking while you read this book?

"Why didn't I try a different medical treatment for my loved one's disease?"

"Why wasn't I there to stop the event from happening?"

"Why didn't I try harder? Fight longer?"

We will address questions like these in a future chapter pertaining to roadblocks we might find along the journey of grief. But for the time being, once again I beseech you:

Please forgive yourself.

There is no good that comes from holding yourself hostage. It is the only way you can effectively resume your journey of grief.

I found myself being held hostage – not by unforgiveness of self, but by life's circumstances – as I awoke that awful Friday of Hell Week.

CHAPTER 14

D-Day

FRIDAY, AUGUST 29, 2003

*U*nless it happens to be the thirteenth, Friday has to be one of the favored days of the week. It's usually the last day of work for most – the beginning of the weekend. A time for relaxation; a break from the day-in, day-out routine of an average life. Friday, August 29, 2003, on the other hand, turned out to be ridiculously far from average for us, one of the worst days of our lives.

I title this entry D-Day. I mean no disrespect to armed service members who took part in the horrific battles that occurred on the true D-Day of World War II, nor do I intend to minimize the term by using it here. But our D-Day proved to be truly horrific for Jenna and me. What does our "D" stand for? Two words – decision and dark.

Friday began like the previous few days had. We woke up from a broken night's "rest" only to enter the nightmare that had been our waking hours for the last few days. Faith was still strong – but who in their right mind *wants* to have these experiences in which to exercise their faith? Yet our faith was all we had, and our faith was essential in guiding us through the next few hours.

Friday was but a few hours old for us before doctors notified us that Micah's condition had significantly worsened. In Chapter 9, I described it as thus: "Oddly enough, when injured brain cells begin to die, they trigger swelling in the brain. Increased brain swelling leads to increased pressure." Well, to continue the story, increased pressure induces more brain cell death. More brain cell death triggers more brain swelling. More swelling increases pressure furthermore. It creates a positive feedback loop of sorts – each brain cell that dies further adds to the problem, amplifying the end result. The bottom line: brain cells were dying exponentially, and brain cells do not regenerate.

Micah's medical team asked to call a meeting with us. We asked if our family could be present at the meeting; in so doing, not only could they be informed, but they would have the opportunity to ask questions that we might not think of. The medical team consented, and a short while later, we met.

Present were a few friends and many members of our family (our parents and grandparents alike). Micah's neurosurgeon was present along with one or two intensivists (Pediatric Intensive Care doctors). They took time out of their day to carefully explain the biological and physiological processes behind Micah's condition. They answered any and all questions any of us had. Then they asked us the question we hoped not to hear:

"Do you want to take him off of life support?"

This wasn't some random medical drama on TV. This was our life. It was painfully real. Decision time. The doctors hadn't given up hope. Nor were they trying to free up a bed. They simply relayed to us what led us to this point: Micah was dying.

They didn't demand answers right away. They gave us all the time in the world to ponder this decision. They encouraged us to go and pray. They encouraged us not to rush into a decision. They provided all the counsel we could want. They encouraged us to seek any and all other counsel we could use. If you ever have to go through something like this, these are the people you want taking care of your loved one.

The medical professionals left the room. They left us with our family. We all sat in silence. What can anyone say? Someone quietly spoke up, "Do what you have to do." Little was spoken amongst us all. Again, this wasn't a TV medical drama; family members didn't start arguing over the "right" choice, throwing chairs and throwing punches. They all, to a person, loved us, supported us, and generally said, "This is your son – do what is best for Micah and for you."

We left the room and went to the "healing gardens" – a beautiful garden on the hospital campus, complete with running waterfall and all – to pray and determine what must be done.

Before I go further, please allow me to take a detour at this point. Jenna and I had been Christians for many years prior to this moment. We both went through a two-year Bible College and ministry training program at our church in the Seattle area. Our home church there was a very faith-based church. "Believe and you shall receive" sums it up nicely. The family from our church with whom we walked on this journey the month prior chose to "stand in faith" – they were determined that their child would walk out of the hospital to great testimony to the Lord. And that would be a great testimony, wouldn't it?

To take a person off of life support, in the eyes of *some* faith-based persons, is tantamount to blasphemy. The act is practically equivalent to abortion in the eyes of some, to be sure. How dare we take life into our own hands? That's God's realm – for Him to decide alone. Keeping that background in the back of your mind, let's return to that moment.

We walked down to the gardens and sat down on a bench in front of the previously mentioned waterfall. Our decision was easy. To be quite honest, we both had "the answer" before our butts met the bench. Our eyes met. Without speaking a word, we knew what had to be done.

We had to let Micah go.

We stayed at those gardens for some time. We wept. We sobbed. We talked. We prayed. We thanked God for our friends and family. We thanked God for Micah's medical team. We also knew how "popular" this decision would be with some of our close friends back at our old "home church." We knew we were about to go against the grain. But we also knew, at that moment, that we were 100% in the right.

You see, we didn't give up on Micah. We still believed God could work a miracle. We also firmly believed that God did not require Micah to be on life support in order to work that miracle. And most importantly, we prayed in earnest for that miracle. But we also believed from Day 1 that all we had in that hospital was a shell – Micah's shell. His soul, his essence – *he* – was in heaven. The sights he must have seen... The experience of being in the presence of the Almighty... How could we take him away from that? The Lord would have to be the One to give him back to us if that was His will.

Parents are charged with doing the very best to take the very best care of their son or daughter. It's no easy task, as any parent knows and will readily tell you. But the irony in our situation was this: in order to take the very best care of Micah, we had to let him go.

We came back from that meeting in the gardens with such a peace. In the midst of this nightmare – *finally* – there was peace. We wouldn't be spared from the pain, the agony, or the frustrations of what was to come, but the Lord would be there with us every step of the way, holding our hands, and comforting us. This was a faith we had never known to this degree previously; a faith that existed deep within the darkest corners of our hearts, a faith without any iota of evidence in the physical realm. At least, so we thought.

As was relayed to us sometime much later, a family friend told us about a particular moment that happened shortly after we returned from the gardens. In this moment, Jenna leaned her back against a wall in the intensive care unit. I embraced her. And behind us stood a third person, comforting us both. This family friend witnessed this from some distance down the hall, and later asked who was with us in that moment, as there were many friends and family that had been with us during this entire ordeal. When we later confirmed that no one was with us in that moment, that it had been only Jenna and me in an embrace, that no friend or family member had stood with us, the family friend told us all what she saw, much to the encouragement of those that heard.

Shortly after returning from the gardens, we first told our family, then the doctors, that we planned to take him off of life support. We would do so the next day – Saturday. This would give time for family members to spend time with him if they desired. This would give us the opportunity to not "rush into things" and spend quality time with, for lack of a better term, Micah's body. (This sounds very odd, I know. But no matter how much we believed our son was already in heaven, his body still provided a strong point of connection to the Micah we knew and loved.) But most importantly, this still allowed time for the miracle we desperately hoped and prayed for. God has raised people from the dead; He certainly could raise someone from the living.

By that afternoon, we were partaking in a ministry the hospital has for those who are about to have a loved one die. A person specializing in "music thanatology" – a subspecialty of palliative care that unites music with medicine – played a harp in Micah's room – music to heal the soul. We made impressions of his hands and feet in plaster. We cut a lock of his hair. We did all of this in the presence of family and friends, and all with the hope that God would still work His miracle.

Later that night, we gave Micah his last bath. From the moment of his arrival in the PICU, Micah had nothing but his diaper on. That night we put *his* clothes back on. He got to look like a little boy again – albeit a far cry from the little boy we ran with, played with, watched videos with, read books to...

As exhausting as the day had been, we both knew that sleep wouldn't come easy again. When your expectations are for little rest, you sometimes are pleasantly surprised by the amount you actually receive, regardless of how little. We laid our heads on our pillows that night praying for a miracle, but ready to face the daunting task of "letting go" if the expected miracle never came.

CHAPTER 15

Miracles Abound

*R*ight now, as I begin to write this chapter, when I consider the word "miracles," my mind immediately jumps to one thing – Easter eggs. Probably not the first image that comes to your mind.

Maybe I can change that by the end of this chapter.

The first reason I so readily link Easter with miracles is based on the reason why Easter is celebrated in the first place – to commemorate the greatest miracle in all of human history: the resurrection of Jesus Christ.

Yet I take it one step further and associate miracles with

Easter eggs – hard-boiled, dyed, candy-filled plastic – it doesn't matter.

As countless other families, churches, and community organizations have done long before us, Jenna and I established an annual tradition for our children. Every year on Easter, we have the Great Miller Easter Egg Hunt.

One year, we shared this hunt with a family near and dear to our hearts. But most other years, the participants are limited to our nuclear family, as well as any grandparents that care to join in the fun. Our backyard, though less than one-third of an acre in size, is large enough to hide enough Easter eggs that, once found, will fill each of our children's Easter buckets to overflowing. We are fortunate enough right now to have children young enough that they do not remember all of our hiding places from year-to-year.

Yet if I'm honest with you, I look forward to this hunt just as much as, if not more than, our children. I look forward to concealing as many eggs as possible, to prepping the yard "just so," and to announce the beginning of the hunt.

Each of our children, worked to a frenzy of anticipation, nervously stand behind one another in single file. Mouths froth over, eyes glaring at the closed back door blinds as if they could see right through them, targeting where each and every prized egg might be found. They are polite; they do not push and shove one another. They know there are enough to go around, and then some.

Yet every muscle in their little bodies tense, every reflex is brought to the forefront, in order that they will be ready to pounce on those hapless little eggs when Mommy and Daddy say...

GO!

The door is thrown open, blinds without time to do the same, and the hounds are released into the wild.

Then comes my favorite part. Each child, acting as if they have been purposefully starved of all nourishment and sweets for the month before, actively searches out and captures each unsuspecting egg. They gather them to themselves like squirrels storing nuts for an upcoming harsh winter.

If only getting them to pick up their rooms was so easy.

But this, my friend, is why Easter eggs reminds me of miracles.

Throughout this account of my journey of grief, I have made several references to praying for miracles. I prayed for my son to be healed. I prayed for my son to be spared. I prayed that my son would return to me in the way I knew him before our nightmare began. I ardently and earnestly prayed for miracles from the Lord I know and love.

These are miracles certainly worth asking for. And as you have likely guessed by now, the miracles I asked for never came. My son was not healed, not spared, and was not returned to me as I had hoped.

Yet I contend that miracles can be found every single day if you and I look hard enough… if, like my children hunting Easter eggs, we actively search them out.

After Micah's death almost a decade ago, having occurred two months before our fourth anniversary, Jenna and I are still married – more in love with one another now than we have been any moment before.

Miracle found.

I have had numerous opportunities to share my experience with others, doing my best to help them along their own journey of grief after the death of a loved one.

Miracle found.

I am sitting here, feeling as far from an expert in my field as I possibly could, writing a book that will (God and publishers willing) further help you and others like you on your own personal journeys.

Miracle found.

Walking out our faith in that hospital room during Hell Week encouraged numerous nurses, doctors, and other medical professionals involved in our son's care.

Miracle found.

At the time of his death, Micah was our one and only child. We didn't know if we could *emotionally* handle bringing any more children into this world. Yet I'm happy to say that since Micah, we have been blessed with the arrivals of Owen, Amelia, Peyton and Ava – four more little lives to enrich our humble life.

Miracle – no – *miracles* found.

So I ask you, where are the miracles that surely exist all around you? Where will you find the next miracle hiding in wait, eager to be discovered, and surely sweeter than any candy-filled Easter egg?

What is that? You think you might have trouble finding them? Well, in that case, can I help you find the first one?

When I was in my labor and delivery class in nursing school, I was shocked to find out just how difficult it is for a human life to be conceived and carried to birth. Although I can't find my specific notes from that day, I found similar facts in an online article titled "The Miracle of Conception."[1] Most of these facts will be reproduced as they appear in the article. Wrap your mind around these, if you can. Every time I read them, they still boggle my mind. (And please remember, as I warned you before, I call things as they are; if your parents told you babies are delivered by storks, you might want to skip some of the following details).

— *Typically, a man's ejaculate [never thought you'd read this word in a book about grief, did you?] holds over 100 million sperm, of which less than 40 million (40,000,000) are considered viable candidates for egg fertilization.*

— *Over the course of their journey to the egg, hazardous traveling conditions violently slashes 40,000,000 viable sperm down to 50 (fifty!) sperm with a chance to fertilize the egg.*

— *The female egg, ever the hospitable host, is only available for fertilization for 12 to 24 hours. If the sperm miss this window, fertilization does not take place.*

— *If the miracle of fertilization takes place, the cells still need to undergo division and implantation, adhering to the uterine wall. If the dividing cells find a uterine wall upon which to affix themselves, the game is still far from over.*

— *The risk of miscarriage is highest immediately after implantation. It is thought that up to half (1 in 2) of all fertilized eggs do not survive, often passed from the uterus in what appears to be a normal period.*

— *Of the fifty percent of fertilized eggs that survive immediately after implantation, it is estimated that up to twenty percent (1 in 5) of known pregnancies will end in miscarriage.*

Your first miracle, my friend, is simply this:
Your life.
The miracle of life turns out to be exactly that – a miracle. Your life, the fact that you live, breathe, and are able to read this book, is a miracle.

And since I'm feeling particularly warm and fuzzy, I'll give you your second miracle for free:
Your loved one's life.
The very fact that your loved one – the one whom you miss more than anything or anyone else on this earth right now, the one who once occupied a very precious place in your life – the fact that they ever came to be created is one of the greatest miracles of all.

Armed with that knowledge, dear friend, go out and hunt down those other miracles. They will strengthen you more than you know.

(Endnote)

1 From an article written by Fiona Baker, found at http://www.birth.com.au/Getting-Pregnant/Conceiving/How-conception-works/The-miracle-of-conception

CHAPTER 16

The Beginning of a Very Long End

SATURDAY, AUGUST 30, 2003

The sun rose bright and shining on Saturday morning. Kids all across the country would wake up, grab a bowl of their favorite cereal, and watch their favorite Saturday morning cartoons. Some might not even make it out of their PJ's before the afternoon. Saturday: a reprieve from school work, from adult work, from major commitments, obligations, or decisions.

Oh, to have a Saturday morning like that.

One week prior to this Saturday, the day before the accident, Jenna woke early and left our apartment to earn money by cleaning house for someone, just as she had done for many weeks prior. I was left with the charge of feeding, clothing, and spending quality time with Micah. I'll be quite honest with you – I *never* enjoyed feeding, changing, and clothing Micah. These were mundane tasks that simply needed to be done because my child needed them to be done. Nor were these always easy tasks, especially when one considers the inexperience that came with Micah being my first child.

But the "spending quality time" part was the one I looked forward to every week. I would play with him with his toys, brainwash him with Major League Baseball DVDs, or generally just lounge around and love on him. I never once thought of doing anything else on a weekend, but I certainly took those moments for granted. How was I to know that one week later, we would stand at his bedside, *in a hospital*, ready to do the unthinkable?

Yet that was the harsh reality of this particular Saturday morning. No miracle. No improvement. All that was left was us, the Lord, and this matter of "letting go." We asked the doctors how long they thought he would live after removing him from life support. They made sure to emphasize that everyone's bodies are different, but given his current condition, they estimated he would live for 20 minutes to 2 hours at the most.

We were in no hurry. Grandparents, family members, even some of our closer friends all went in and had their last moments with him. When all had said their good-byes and left the room to sob and mourn and wait for his actual death, we were ready. The curtains were drawn; the doors were shut. A very lovely, lovely nurse named Kristy, an angel masquerading as a nurse, a nurse who personified what it meant to be a nurse, a nurse who had cared for Micah the night before, agreed to stay extra hours over her shift to remove him from life support. Jenna was to hold him. I would be at her side. It would be just the four of us – caregiver, parents, and Micah.

The emotions we felt – the pain, the anguish, the "rawness" of it all – peaked. Now was the time we would watch our beloved son – only child, product of our flesh and God's beauty – die. Words cannot describe the pain. There is nothing in the English language, or any language for that matter.

Kristy removed Micah from life support – feeding tube and all – and placed him in Jenna's arms. His lifeless body, limp in her arms, was at once altogether beautiful and horrifying. Micah, but not Micah. And at any moment now, he would be gone.

Jenna's body heaved with sobs that I pray I never have to hear again. What was going through her mind and heart I couldn't know for certain. I, however, sat there experiencing an anguish unlike any I've felt before, feeling as though my very soul was being torn in two, thinking that despite the magnitude of my pain, this must be just one infinitesimal amount compared to the anguish God the Father felt when He watched His only Son die on a cross – but I could now, in some small way, blasphemous as it may be, relate to that moment in history. This thought also caused immediate humility within. After all, my son did not sacrifice himself as Jesus did. Yet, in a way, he was a sacrifice. His was the body that took the brunt of the impact; his was the head that dented that windshield. The father in me screamed that it should be me who was dying, me who was removed from life support... why my son, who had exuded such vibrant life for a brief sixteen months? Why my son, who lived without really living, without experiencing all that life had to offer? I'd lived plenty, had so many opportunities to impact others... Why couldn't it have been me lying there?

The minutes felt like hours. Then those minutes that felt like hours did something we hadn't anticipated – they *became* hours. The climactic finale to this drawn-out ordeal at once became anti-climactic. Our emotions – all the pain, suffering, anguish, internal turmoil – crashed. A new nightmare had been birthed. Why wasn't he dying? Did we make the right decision? Was God working a last minute miracle? What was going on?

We asked these questions of the medical staff taking care of Micah. Doctors explained that Micah's brain stem – the part of the brain responsible for basic functions such as breathing and circulation – kicked in and started working. His brain stem was located far from the dying brain cells. It did what it was created to do – keep on keepin' on.

As time slowly dragged on, grandparents and great-grandparents came back in one at a time or two at a time to hold him. Jenna and I, not wanting to miss the moment of his death, lingered nearby – sometimes in his room, sometimes in a waiting room. How long would this last? Was he suffering? What literally in God's gracious name was going on?

We continued to consult with the intensivists on-duty that day. They reassured us that sometimes this happens – they've seen it before. They also explained that although they have no definitive way to tell, all research pointed to the fact that the patient in this situation does not suffer. There are no signs or symptoms of pain. Pain is registered by the very brain cells that were dying. The brain stem was, as described before, simply doing its thing – keeping the body alive as long as possible.

As day stretched into night, it became very evident that Micah's body was going to once again contradict what doctors thought would happen. On Wednesday they thought he would get better; instead he got worse. Today they thought he would die quickly; yet his body continued to live. Would God work His miracle after all? Do we pray for the miracle? Or do we now pray for a quick, timely death?

Our weary souls needed rest. The emotional upheaval experienced that day brought along a fatigue that touched every aspect of our beings. It's funny; many people go to sleep at night hoping and praying that nightmares won't visit them as they do so. It became common practice for us, however, to hope to sleep in order to *escape* the nightmare that was our waking life. And despite all of the questions that wracked our minds, questions both old and new that currently came without answers, as we once again attempted to sleep that night, one thing was certain:

Our nightmare was far from over.

CHAPTER 17

Yelling at God

I still remember it – *feel it* – as if it happened only yesterday. As I mentioned at the beginning of the previous chapter, Jenna often worked on Saturday mornings, cleaning the home of a family friend. The first Saturday that she returned to work after Micah's death, I was left home alone without my little man to play with. That Saturday marked a very low point for me.

I lied curled up in a ball on the couch, my body shaking with sobs, wishing it had been me who died instead of Micah. The pain of having my one and only boy seemingly ripped from me permeated every fiber of my being. My heart hurt, not only figuratively and emotionally, but *physically* hurt, as if every strand of heart muscle acknowledged the hole that existed in the place where only the love for my boy once took residence.

I screamed and yelled at God for not taking me instead, for not being there, for not stopping the accident, for allowing me to come to such a wretched place in my life. My pain was so great, my roaring at God so loud, I was surprised police officers hadn't shown up at my door to stop whatever crime my neighbors surely thought I was in the midst of committing. At no time did I ever feel suicidal, as I have always valued life too greatly; but in that moment I came closest to knowing what that feeling would "taste" like. In that moment I recognized what brings people to that point of desperation. So instead of harming myself, I continued to simply lie there...

...and yell.

In the midst of your journey of grief, have you ever felt like that? Have you ever wanted to yell at God? Have you ever wanted to tell Him off? Have you actually done it? I'm going to let you in on a little secret, one that I hope will not prevent you from reading the rest of this chapter, allowing me to explain myself fully:

Secret #1: It's okay to yell at God.

Not only is it okay to yell at God, but I actually recommend yelling at God if you are angry and feel so inclined. How is it that a Bible-believing, Jesus-loving man who calls himself a

Christian comes to argue *in favor* of yelling at God? Easy.

I've done it.

And I've lived to tell about it.

A simple examination of my body will bear evidence to the fact that I have not one thunderbolt singe mark anywhere from head to toe. I have yet to be driven into the earth like a human nail, smashed upon the head with a proverbial celestial hammer. I am smitten with the Lord, but have yet to be smitten by Him.

And far more important than any of these things, I draw your attention to something I stated in Chapter 4, something so important that it bears repeating here: my faith is not in organized religion (man's attempt to relate with God), but in relationship (God's attempt to relate with man). As I read the Bible, I find a God who has been and always will be actively attempting to relate with His creation. This is evident in His relationship with Adam and Eve, in the covenant He made with good ol' Father Abraham, in yet another covenant He made with Noah, in the birth, life, death, and resurrection of His son Jesus Christ, all the way up to the present day and beyond.

It is because of this very relational heart of God that I recommend yelling at Him when the pain is so great, when anger is all that exists before your vision.

First of all, taking this argument logically, if you yell at a God that doesn't exist, you have still effectively provided an outlet by which you can vent your anger and pain, all without bringing harm to yourself or others.

But better yet, if God *does* exist, you are taking a step in relating with Him, even in the midst of your pain. And when you have a relationship with the Creator of the universe... with the One who knows you better than you know yourself... who better is there to help you on your journey of grief?

Convinced? If so, take a moment to set this book down, open those lungs God gave you, and give a hearty yell. Seriously. I mean it. I'll wait for you right here. Go ahead and clear that chest that has been burdened for far too long. (Well, unless you're on a public bus or in some other location that might invite the presence of the aforementioned friendly police officers. In that case, you might want to wait a little while longer before giving this exercise a try.)

Done? Feel better? No? Ohhh... you're not much of a yeller, you say. Okay, I get that. Then please allow me to take this whole yelling thing one step further. (Those of you who just yelled your guts out can stuff them back in and also take note of the next secret I want to share with you.)

Secret #2: It's okay to question God.

For those of you that audibly gasped, I'm sorry. But really, don't we humans question Him daily, even if said questions aren't directed at Him? Take some of the following questions for example:

"Why do I strive so hard, often times seemingly for nothing?"

"Why can life be so difficult?"

"What have I done to You, God? Why have You set me as Your target?!"

"Why do bad people live and become old, some even mighty in power?!"

"WHY DID OUR MICAH HAVE TO DIE?!"

Okay – that last question was mine. But have you ever asked questions like these? Ever *felt* like asking questions like these? When it comes right down to it, these questions and the scores more like them all boil down to one essential question that humans have been asking for millennia:

Why is it that a God that is supposedly loving, ever-present, all-knowing, and all-powerful allows such horrible things to happen on this dirtball of a planet we call home?

Sure, I might be paraphrasing it a bit. Yet how many times have we heard or asked variances of this very same question? God knows the opportunities to do so abound. Read any headline on any given day and you can find so many opportunities to ask the question *WHY?*

When a mother or father murders their children, their spouse, then commits suicide...

...when a pilot, driver, or captain crashes a plane, car, or boat, killing innocent people...

...when a tsunami, earthquake, or other natural disaster levels cities, destroying lives...

...when your loved one succumbs to the illness they so voraciously battled, or is killed, accidentally or intentionally...

...when my beautiful little boy, seemingly with so many decades of life ahead of him, dies after being hit by a van...

All of these events – readily occurring on a daily basis – can cause us to question the existence of any god at all, let alone the God referred to in the Bible. The "Why Does God Allow Bad Things to Happen" question is one that is often used as evidence against the existence of God, and one that humankind has wrestled with long before and after you and I have walked and drawn breath on this earth.

Needless to say, and sorry to disappoint you, but I can't provide a definitive answer to it. If I could, I would best all of the great philosophers in human history, likely selling a great number of books along the way. Nay, I'm just a humble little father navigating the journey of grief, tucked away in a corner of the United States of America, but one that will at least say his two cents worth regarding the matter just the same.

In regards to this matter of questioning God, and in particular the previously mentioned all-knowing, ever-present all-powerful God of the Bible, of asking the great question *WHY?*, I shall progress by presenting and answering three questions of my own.

Question #1: WHY? Why ask why?

Let me rephrase the question. Why do we, as human beings, ask questions? The simple answer: *because we need answers*. Questions are asked when answers are needed.

And why is it, dear friend, that we need answers? We need answers because *we're not God*. We don't know everything. We didn't create the earth, the universe, and all that it contains.

Taking it one step further, *if we didn't need answers, we wouldn't need God*. And this brings us right back to the relational aspect of God I wrote about earlier. I believe God specifically created us with an incredible *hunger* for answers, for knowledge, and for understanding. I emphasize the word hunger for good reason.

We all know the Bible story of Adam and Eve, right? If not, here is a brief recap. God created Adam and Eve, pointed out a particular tree commanding them not to eat its fruit, only to have Satan show up in the form of a serpent, tempting Eve to eat the forbidden fruit, who in turn tempted Adam to eat, thereby forever changing their intimate relationship with God, essentially causing all of the problems mankind faces today.

Thanks a lot, Adam and Eve.

It is in this most basic of Bible stories, however, that we see God establishing what He desired to be His relationship with His creation – you and me. For a long time, this Biblical account of Adam and Eve bothered me. I felt as if mankind was set up to fail from the very beginning, as if God delighted in singling out one fruit in all the Garden, said "don't touch," then waited behind a bush, giggling at the inevitable outcome of His decree – our disobedience, and our inevitable punishment.

But this couldn't be further from the truth. In this account we see his desire to give us free will. He didn't force us to love and obey Him; He wanted us – from the very beginning – to *choose* to obey Him. But why the tree? Why the "do not eat" instruction?

The answer lies in the particular tree that God singled out. It is referred to as the tree of the knowledge of good and evil.[1] God did not want man to eat the fruit of that tree. Why? Did He want to keep us stupid? Hardly. I believe the answer is simple:

He wants us to come to Him when we hunger for knowledge.

That's all He wanted from Adam and Eve in the first place. I see this with my own children. Even in childhood, they have questions about life, about the world around them. There are many modern day sources they can seek out on their own to discover the answers to their questions, but I would much rather them seek the answers from me; when they do so, we can find the answers to their questions together, and in so doing, strengthen our own relationship with each other.

Like a good father with his children, God invited Adam and Eve to come to Him when they had questions. But in order to choose Him, they needed an alternate that could also be chosen; in their case, it was the fruit of the tree of knowledge of good and evil.

When the serpent tempted Eve to eat the fruit, he did so by telling her that it would open her eyes, making her *like God*, knowing good and evil.[2]

Our hunger for knowledge, for answers, will cause us to do one of two things. We will either seek answers apart from God, becoming *like God*, or we will seek answers from God Himself, causing us to become *closer to God*. There are many questions for which we will find answers in textbooks and knowledge already gathered by humankind. In my nursing profession, if I want to know how to administer a particular medication, I simply look up that medication in a drug handbook, either in print or on the computer.

But if I seek answers to questions that are infinitely deeper than how to administer a medication – like "Why did my son have to die?" – then I am reasonably sure that there is no text that will contain the specific answers I seek. It is in those moments that I will freely question God, and it is in similar moments I encourage you to do the same.

So why do we ask why? We ask why because we are created to do so, in order that we might have a closer relationship with an all-knowing and loving God.

Question #2: WHO? Who asks why?

This question also has a simple answer: everyone. I try to avoid extremes, but in this case I believe it is applicable. I can't imagine there has been or ever will be a single human being in all the earth that doesn't have a question they need or want answered. This hunger for knowledge of which I speak is universal. Some people want to know how things work. Others want to know why someone doesn't love them back.

But for the purposes of this chapter, I am specifically asking who might ask the question of WHY – the one that started this entire section – the deep longing to know why a good God could allow evil and suffering in the world.

Anyone could ask this question of WHY. Many of us do, myself included. But in the same book that describes an all-knowing and loving God, there are many examples of people throughout history who have questioned God. I would like to highlight three of them here.

King David

You know David, right? The shepherd. The Israelite who killed Goliath with a smooth stone and a sling. The one who would rise to prominence and become the second king of Israel. The adulterer, causing the entire Bathsheba affair. In the Bible, God Himself refers to David as a man after His heart.[3]

And yet this man after God's own heart questions God on more than one occasion. He asks God why He sleeps[4], why He forgets David's affliction and oppression[5], why He stands far away[6], and my personal favorite, why He hides Himself in times of trouble[7].

If a man described by God as being after God's own heart can question God, why can't you and I?

Job

Ah, Job. Remember him? He's the poster boy for all things suffering and grief. It would be practically sacrilegious to *not* mention Job in a book about grief.

The Bible describes Job in similar terms as David, being "blameless and upright, one who feared God and turned away from evil."[8] He has ten children, all of whom die tragically *simply because God let Satan kill them*.[9] Yet, as you read the entirety of the book of Job, you see that this "blameless and upright" man, this man who "did not sin or charge God with wrong,"[10] questions God throughout the entire book, bringing up more WHY questions per minute than one would think is humanly possible. Here is but a sample of his questions, a few of which you already read (paraphrased) many paragraphs before:

"Why did I not die at birth, come out from the womb and expire?" (Job 3:11)

"Why is light given to him who is in misery, and life to the bitter in soul..." (Job 3:20)

"What do I do to you, you watcher of mankind? Why have you made me your mark? Why have I become a burden to you?" (Job 7:20)

"Why do you not pardon my transgression and take away my iniquity?" (Job 7:21)

"Why then do I labor in vain?" (Job 9:29)

"...let me know why you contend against me." (Job 10:2)

"Why do you hide your face and count me as your enemy?" (Job 13:24)

"Why do the wicked live, reach old age, and grow mighty in power?" (Job 21:7)

"...why do those who know him never see his days?" (Job 24:1)

And yet despite his persistent (and I believe justified) questioning of God throughout his entire ordeal, his account ends with his latter days being more blessed than his beginning, given more possessions, having more children, and living long enough to see his future offspring up to four generations.[11]

Jesus Christ

Yes, even Jesus Christ, the very Son of God, described in the Bible as being completely sinless and without blame, questioned God the Father. While He was dying on the cross, He asked, "My God, My God, why have You forsaken Me?"[12]

Feeling more encouraged yet? If these three men can question God, I see no reason why we cannot. Just know that when we do so, we must keep the answers to this last question in mind:

Question #3: WHAT? What is God's reply?

When we ask God WHY, He may or may not reply. It is entirely His prerogative. He enabled King David to praise

Him in the midst of questioning Him. He replied both directly and very matter-of-factly to Job, and then blessed him like crazy. And as best as we can tell, there is nothing in the Bible that mentions Him responding to Jesus on the cross.

Although He may or may not respond to our specific queries, and taking into account His character as described in the Bible, I believe there are five key "general replies" that He might give in place of concrete answers. These five replies are universal in nature, and can be utilized by you and me in our pursuit of the answers we desperately seek.

1) Don't stop asking questions.

As a student nurse, I remember at one time thinking to myself, "I can't wait until I've practiced as a nurse long enough to no longer need to ask all these questions of other nurses." Guess what? I've practiced as a full-time nurse almost seven years now, and I'm *still* asking questions. My peers do as well. Sure, part of this has to do with the ever-changing healthcare industry we are a part of. But we ask questions even when we think we should know the answer, even when we've asked the same question before. Why? Because communication is essential if we are going to function as a team, offering the very best care we can in the process. It allows us to prevent isolation, stagnation, and as a result, poor care.

It also allows us to relate to one another.

When we stop asking Him questions, we stop relating to Him. He's a big God – He can handle any question we throw His way. There are multiple scriptures in the Bible admonishing us to ask Him questions. Keep in mind there are often benefits to asking God questions:

"Do not be anxious about anything, but in everything by prayer and supplication with thanksgiving let your requests be made known to God. And the peace of God, which surpasses all understanding, will guard your hearts and your minds in Christ Jesus."[13]

I don't know about you, but when Micah died, I often found peace hard to come by. Come to think of it, this can actually be said of normal day-to-day life for that matter!

2) Don't fear asking questions.

Novelist Madeleine L'Engle said it best:

"If my religion is true, it will stand up to all my questioning; there is no need to fear."[14]

If a real relationship with God is to be had, it will stand up to any questions you might have for Him.

3) Don't forget about free will.

The free will given to Adam and Eve extends to all of humanity. Sometimes the things that happen in life are simply a result of the fact that we have each been given that free will. When Micah died, Jenna and I of course asked the standard questions: "Why? Why us? Why now? Why Micah?" And although we haven't had the pleasure of receiving answers to these questions directly from God, and quite possibly never will this side of heaven, I am not of the belief that either Satan killed or God took our son.

Instead, I believe our journey of grief started when two separate families made choices birthed from free will – we chose to go on a walk, the family that hit us chose to go for a drive – that produced a result outside of anything we could have ever imagined that day, the death of our Micah.

4) Don't stop trusting God.

Having never received a direct answer from God as to why our son died, I can say only one thing with certainty. Our son's death did not change God's character. Believing in, following, and loving God does not preclude tragedy from entering your life. Trust Him in all things, even when life takes a turn you never saw coming, and especially while you continue to question Him.

5) Don't give up hope.

One of my favorite scriptures is found in Galatians:

"And let us not grow weary of doing good, for in due season we will reap, if we do not give up."[5]

In the context of questioning God, how is it possible to grow weary and lose heart? We can do so in one of two ways: 1) by not asking God the burning WHY questions, which will cause them to inevitably weigh you down, or 2) by asking the WHY questions without trusting God regardless of His answer, or lack thereof. If you avoid these two things while questioning God, you can do so while maintaining the hope that will be an ever-present help on your journey of grief.

Lastly, all of this talk about yelling at God and questioning God makes me think of my own children. If my children are mad at me (and I *really* have to work hard to imagine what that would be like), I would rather they communicate with me, talking with me (or yelling at me) about their problems, in order that we might work together on our relationship. I had a hand in creating them. They are part of me. I love them more than almost anything else on this planet. I would be devastated if their anger toward me caused a break in our relationship.

The same is true of God. He is real, He created you, and He loves you more than you know. In the interest of cultivating a relationship with Him, talk with Him, question Him, and yell at Him if need be.

He's there for you.

And He's been there for me.

And on the Sunday after our accident, the eighth day of our Hell Week, I needed Him more than I ever have before or since.

(Endnotes)

1   Genesis 2:17
2   Genesis 3:5
3   Acts 13:22
4   Psalm 44:23
5   Psalm 44:24
6   Psalm 10:1
7   Psalm 10:1 and Psalm 44:24
8   Job 1:1
9   Job 1:9-19
10 Job 1:22
11 Job 42:12-16
12 Matthew 27:46
13 Philippians 4:6-7
14 http://www.quotationspage.com/quote/33286.html
15 Galatians 6:9

CHAPTER 18

The Lord's Day

SUNDAY, AUGUST 31, 2003

It's hard to explain, really. When we woke Sunday morning to discover no change in Micah's status, we didn't know what to feel. Anguish and pain are difficult enough. Confusion added to the mix makes a big ol' mess of things. His body continued to live. It begged the natural question, "Did we do the right thing?" Yet, anytime a thought like that crossed our minds, the peace we experienced before was there. A peace that told us we were indeed doing the right thing. Doubt and assurance practically mixed into a cocktail that was bitter at first, but left a sweet aftertaste. It was a cocktail we would taste several times over the next little while.

Yet I had to know. I requested a repeat CAT scan to determine if his brain cells were continuing their death-march, or if God was possibly healing his brain. As much as the Lord's peace helped, I wasn't about to balk at a man-made opportunity to catch a glimpse at what was going on.

The CAT scan was completed without question. Contrary to normal protocol, a radiologist came to the floor personally to show us the findings. He allowed, at our request, a few of our family and friends to gather as he pulled up the pictures of Micah's brain. The repeat CAT scan proved what I already knew in my heart – his brain was dying more and more every hour. The radiologist compared that morning's CAT scan to one done a day or two prior – the advancing brain-cell death was undeniable. God's miracle had not come.

Buoyed by these findings, Jenna and I continued our vigil. We simply couldn't miss the moment of Micah's death. Fortunately for us, my father-in-law had set up a "vigil" of sorts as well. It was agreed upon by various family members that they would take "shifts" holding Micah's body. From the moment Jenna and I held his body when we took him off of life support less than 24 hours earlier to the moment he died, he would always be held. How important was that when we believed he was in heaven already? Again, his body was the last connection we had to him – it mattered.

As the day progressed, we had many more "cocktails" of doubt and assurance. As if able to detect our feelings, a lovely,

lovely doctor, one of the pediatric intensivists, took us aside into a small and cozy family conference room of sorts. Dr. Fry gently asked, "How are you doing?" This doctor had experience, knowledge, and passion – yet she never lost her heart for her patients. And we benefited from her kindness that day.

I'll never forget our conversation. After advancing from generalities to specifics, the subject ultimately rested on one major personal burden – the feeding tube (or lack thereof). I timidly asked the simple question in the form of a statement, "At least we're not euthanizing him." She responded with the truth, "Well, technically, you are passively euthanizing Micah." My heart sunk to my stomach. We *were* killing him after all. We had been told a couple of days prior that the hospital's ethics committee had met, that there was unanimous agreement in regards to our situation and our choice of action. No board of ethics, however, could alleviate what I felt in that microsecond – we were killing Micah. Completely unaware of my thoughts (or perhaps not?), she looked me straight in the eyes, and with fervor I had not felt before, she continued, "But remember one thing. You are *not* killing your son. The van that hit him is what killed him. Without that, you aren't here in this situation today. Don't ever forget that."

As He had done all week long in various ways using various people, God used Dr. Fry in that moment to speak into our lives. The burden instantaneously lifted, what I hoped would be once and for all.

That, however, would not be the case. A little while later, sensing our need for a break from it all (and perhaps smelling the body of a man who hadn't showered in days), our family encouraged us to run back to our apartment and shower. They gave us a cell phone and stated they would call immediately if Micah's condition changed in any way. With some reluctance, we decided to take them up on their gracious offer. The idea of getting some distance was very appealing, not to mention a nice, warm shower – as if the difficulties of the last few days would simply wash away.

When we first walked through the door of our apartment, having not been there at all since we left for that fateful walk six days prior, all at once grief hit and hit hard, like a sucker punch right to the gut. There was Micah's makeshift bedroom in what was supposed to be the living room of our one-bedroom apartment. There were his toys, his quilts, his crib, his highchair, even some small cubes of cheese he had as a pre-walk snack – all staring us in the face and again slamming us in the gut.

Wasn't quite ready for that.

But we came with a mission, and we didn't want to be gone too long, despite the assurances we received from our family. As Jenna had showered at the hospital earlier that morning, I decided I wouldn't waste time to start mine.

Then the house phone rang.

Do you pick it up? What would you say to whoever was calling? (Word had spread fast about our circumstances, as friends who came from the Seattle area were passing along updates to those back at "home.") Jenna answered. It was one of our pastors from the "Westside," one that had been close to both of us in different ways for years. One who knew each of us practically inside and out. And he asked to speak with me.

It's very possible he made small talk, asking us how we were doing and the like. I don't recall that at all, however. What I do remember him asking was, "I hear you've taken Micah off of life support. Is that true?" I replied in the affirmative. His next five words practically felled me to the ground: "What about the feeding tube?" These two questions were quick, abrupt, and rapidly cut to the core of what I was dealing with. Was this the work of the Lord? Did He have us get to our apartment in time if only to take this call? Was I wrong after all? Whatever burden of doubt had been lifted hours earlier came crashing back one-hundred-fold. I feebly uttered that we had it under control (ha-ha) and were doing what we knew (hardy-har-har) was right. I don't recall much small talk after that – the call ended as abruptly as it began. Jenna asked what was wrong. I couldn't speak. I retreated to the safety of the shower, where more than the water from the faucet flowed.

I'd had it. Decisions, doubts, fears, tears, pain more severe than anything I'd ever known before finally had their victory. All I could do was stand in that shower, naked physically, mentally, and emotionally, and weep. The roller coaster stopped. Time stood still as the water and tears flowed. Then, in a voice so clear it was nearly audible, God spoke.

"Who are you accountable to? In this situation, who are you accountable to, Eric?"

I have never heard the audible voice of the Lord – but I also have never heard Him so clearly as in that moment. The answer came almost as quickly as the question. I was responsible to two people and two people only. The first: God Himself. I'm accountable to Him in all things. The second: Micah.

When I too eventually pass from this world to the next, what will Micah say to me? Will he ask, "Why didn't you try harder, Dad?" Or will he simply state, "Thank you – thank you for letting go." It was in that moment that I was imparted with the greatest gift I could receive during this entire ordeal, a gift from God Himself, a simple realization that was the key to how I handled everything from that moment forward:

That it took more faith to let go of Micah than it did to fight for his life.

The tears kept coming – but now they were tears of relief. Tears of gratitude. Tears of praise to the One who holds my past, my present, and my future in His very capable hands. When I finished my shower, I explained everything to Jenna. We were on the right track. Nothing, and I mean *nothing* could sway me now. I knew that whatever time was left in this ordeal would still not be easy. But I also knew that whatever time remained would be doubt-free, gone for good. Now it was a matter of waiting and taking what would come in stride – side-by-side with my one and only Jenna and my one and only Lord.

And I wouldn't have it any other way.

CHAPTER 19

What About God?

Golly. For someone who claimed at the beginning of this book to not Bible-thump you into taking the same journey of grief, I sure do mention God and the Bible a lot don't I?

Can't say I'm going to apologize for it, though.

Yet my original heart still holds true. My goal in writing this book is not to make you a believer. I won't lie – if you weren't one when you started and are one when you're done, I'll be sure to heap praises upon God for that. But it's not my intent to offend or preach you to death.

And yet God is so integrated into my life, into my journey of grief, that I can't help but talk about Him over the course of a couple dozen chapters or so. Truth is, as the previous chapter so perfectly illustrates, I simply have no idea how I would have survived Micah's death if it weren't for Him.

While I'm focused on this subject, please allow me to share with you a pair of thoughts.

Thought #1: Death wasn't part of God's original plan.

If this thing we call life is a party, then death is the unwanted guest. I would like to say "uninvited guest," but that simply isn't true. Who invited death to this party of life? Adam and Eve. Remember when I talked about how Adam and Eve ate the fruit of the tree of knowledge of good and evil? When God warned them about that, He spelled out what would happen very clearly: "...in the day that you eat of it you shall surely die."[1] This was later supported by the Apostle Paul in the New Testament book of Romans when he said, "...one trespass [Adam's] led to condemnation for all men..."[2]

God didn't want death for us. And yet, here we are – death is a very real consequence, invited to the party by a dude we never personally knew. But there's good news!

Thought #2: Death is not the end.

The author of the book of Acts states, "...having a hope in God, which these men themselves accept, that there will be a resurrection of both the just and the unjust."[3]

Furthermore, if you finish the above-quoted Romans scripture, it goes on to say, "...so one act of righteousness [Jesus's] leads to justification and life for all men."[4]

You see my friend, God is real. Some deny His existence. But heck, if you've never met me personally, I suppose you could also deny my existence (and feel free to do so – doesn't bother me one bit, though it might get a little awkward if we ever meet). One problem with that: you're reading my book. And guess what, this God guy has written a book too (one that is far superior to mine in every way, might I add).

He has always been and always will be. Although there are very few parallels between the character of Bob Wiley in the movie *What About Bob* and God Himself, there is one scene I find particularly humorous (okay, many scenes, but for the sake of this chapter, I will only discuss one). Dr. Leo Marvin, frustrated with Bob's antics, kicks Bob out of the house. Dr. Marvin's family complains about Bob being gone. While opening his front door, revealing Bob still standing there, he fires back:

> *"You think he's gone? He's not gone. That's the whole point! He's never gone!"*

That scene makes me laugh every time, but for the sake of this argument, I find it very applicable to God. *You think He's gone? He's not gone. That's the point! He's never gone!* God hasn't abandoned you in your time of need. He's not gone!

He wants a relationship with me. He wants a relationship with you. He could, in His power and might, override our free will and force us to love Him. But forced love – a forced relationship – never works. I didn't win over my beautiful wife by forcing her to love me. Our children might be stuck with us as parents, but we sure can't force them to return our love.

But when they do, I know that they choose to do so, and I can't think of anything sweeter than that.

The same is true of God. He is real, and He will take this journey with you if you allow. You are the one who has to invite Him in, to ask Him to come along with you, so that together you can figure out this process of living after someone you loved has died. If this rings true for you, please go to your local church, your local pastor, or even a friend and tell him or her of your need for God. You can even start things off right now, wherever you might be, by saying a simple prayer. Ask God to forgive you of your sins, invite Jesus Christ into your heart and into your journey of grief.

And then hold on tight, 'cause your bumpy road, though still bumpy, will be far more endurable!

(Endnotes)

1   Genesis 2:17
2   Romans 5:18a
3   Acts 24:15
4   Romans 5:18b

CHAPTER 20

So Close and Yet So Far

MONDAY, SEPTEMBER 1, 2003

Monday marked so many things. It marked the start of a new month. It marked the Labor Day holiday. It marked the "over-one-week" benchmark of our personal hell. It marked a day of reflection. It also marked a day filled with paradoxes – a paradox being any person, thing, or situation exhibiting an apparently contradictory nature.[1]

Micah's condition hadn't changed much from the day

before. His brain stem did what God created it to do. Our family, true to their word, kept up their vigil. Micah's body was held throughout the night. One thing I failed to mention before – Jenna and I were told that at *any time* we wanted to hold Micah, whoever happened to be holding him at the time would surrender him to us. They allowed us to play the "parent card."

Therein lays the first paradox, and quite frankly, the largest of the bunch. Although my faith was rock-solid from the experience I had with God the day before, there still existed different conflicting emotions. Jenna and I wanted more than anything in the world to be with Micah's body at all times – we couldn't stand the thought of missing a thing, or abandoning his physical "shell" during these last days. Yet, simultaneously, we both wanted to run as fast and as far away from that situation as possible. The pain was so great – equally as great as our love for him. One never over-powered the other. I had never experienced it before, and haven't since to this day. Both feelings so powerfully present in my soul simultaneously... it's enough to drive someone mad.

Fortunately for us, we had family and friends that encouraged us to step out from time to time. Always with a cell phone, always never so far as to not be able to come back when the inevitable arrived. On one such occasion, Jenna and I took a walk to Manito Park – a beautiful park not too far from the hospital's campus. We walked hand-in-hand, strolling along the sidewalk as a pair of lovers would; only every step of our walk was made not with steps lightened by love, but heavy steps burdened by grief. We walked a ways into the park, and then laid on the grass – her head resting on my belly.

There, paradox number two quickly became apparent. Our ventures into the "outside world" during Micah's stay at the hospital were few. But we realized that "out here," out in the "real world," life was plugging along as it always had. Families played in the park. People scurried to and fro, some talking on cell phones about some important business or family matter. The Labor Day vacation was in full swing for some. People ate out at restaurants, laughing, smiling, or perhaps just conversing. *None* of these people knew that hell had poured out its fury on two lonely parents. For us, time stood still. Normal life had been placed on "pause" the Sunday before. But for everyone else, life was on "play" – business as usual.

When would it ever go back to "play" for us?

Meanwhile, there were two new developments in Micah's status. The first: "neural cries." A neural cry is a common manifestation present, often in infants and small children, from hypoxia (lack of oxygen)-related central nervous system damage. If I had to choose a word to describe them, "awful" pretty much sums things up. A neural cry is almost like an exaggerated whimper accompanying a sigh. It's unlike any normal child's cry I've ever heard. It doesn't last long, but it doesn't have to. Coming from your child – it's unnerving. It's also, as was explained to us, not uncommon. As if this new development didn't make things uncomfortable enough, along came the second new development. One of Micah's eyes opened. And it would stay that way until moments before his death.

I share these details with you not for shock value, but for perspective. We thought things were as difficult as they were going to be until Micah finally died. We were wrong – *way* wrong. These developments made things far more challenging. Nurses and doctors explained that they had seen these things before. They assured us that these manifestations were reflexive. These manifestations often give parents a false hope that their child is improving, when the exact opposite is true – death is near.

We were coming close to the end.

The doctors explained that there were medications that decrease the frequency of neural cries; these medications were not for the patient, as the patient was not experiencing pain. These medications, while given to the patient, were for the benefit of the parents. We consented to give Micah's body these medications.

I took a turn holding Micah later that night – open eye, neural cries, and all. His body was as lifeless as it had been since the accident. Looking at his face and into this open eye brought about the third paradox of the day. That open eye was still Micah's chocolate brown eye – it had been brown from the day of his birth. Yet this eye I looked into was not the one that, with its partner, shone the light of my dear, sweet boy; rather, it was cold, unmoving, and lifeless. It is difficult to describe how surreal this moment was for me. I knew this was certainly no longer my boy – not in the sense that I knew over the previous sixteen months – yet I couldn't help but still hold him. The physical connection between parent and child is so incredibly powerful. And I knew these opportunities to hold his body wouldn't be around much longer.

Allow me to open a window into some very personal ethical issues at this moment. I've never understood the argument in favor of abortion. But I've never been impregnated by an evil, vile, repulsive attacker, either. Nor had I ever understood the argument in favor of active euthanasia – intentionally inducing the death of a human being – until that moment. As awful as it was to feel, and as awful as it is for me to type, I longed for a way to bring our suffering to an end. I longed for a drug, or even more barbarically, a pillow – anything that could speed this process and end this agony. How's that sound coming from a loving, devoted father?

But it was true. Pain, if strong enough and sustained for long enough periods of time, has great potential to drive a normal, well-balanced person to do things they would never consider doing. In those moments, I never had the desire to act on that longing, but the longing was there just the same. In truth, the longing was fleeting. But it lasted too long for my liking. And I pray to the Lord above that I never have to experience anything that brings that much pain again.

I held Micah for a while longer. I had been invited to take part in an Uno game with my brother-in-law and two very close friends to Jenna and me. Invitations had come before, and I denied every one of them. But that night I accepted. I needed a taste of normalcy.

What quickly ensued was the last paradox of the day. While my precious son's body lay dying next door, I sat in an adjacent room and laughed my head off playing a card game with family and friends. I laughed so hard during that game that tears – tears of laughter – saturated my sorrow-parched face. It was like a sweet rain after a drought – so refreshing, so liberating, and yet the irony of the moment was not lost on me. No guilt – just irony. And if given the same opportunity all over again, I'd accept.

Even if I knew what the next morning was about to bring.

(Endnote)

1   http://dictionary.reference.com/browse/paradox?s=t

CHAPTER 21

Roadblocks on the Journey

*T*here is nothing worse for an author than having steam-rolling progress halted by writer's block (says an author who watched his son take his last breath; suppose I should reconsider this statement). But just the same, writer's block is the bane of any author – new and green or well-established. Often times the block comes from nowhere. *Where does my character go from here? How do I start/end this chapter? How do I resolve this potential problem that has cropped up?*

Take this relatively inexperienced author and this particular chapter, for example. For the last couple of days, I simply couldn't think of the most effective way to lead off this section of information.

Is there a humorous story I can lead off with, something personal from my own life, something that might offset the pain from the previous chapter? Nope.

Oooh, I got it... I can track down a witty story that will tie in perfectly with this subject matter. That will surely get the juices flowing (and possibly impress the reader, too – two birds with one stone!). Nuh-uh.

Alright, I know how to tackle this one. Maybe I'll just discuss the frustrations and philosophical issues that actual physical roadblocks can produce. Are you kidding me?

And then, as if my personal muse flipped a switch and illuminated the solution that was always before my eyes, tauntingly out of reach, it hit me. This writer's block, this issue I wrestled with for a brief couple of days, *this* is what I lead with.

I enjoy writing. I enjoy expressing myself on paper, attempting to do so in such a way that impacts a reader. I enjoy facing the challenges that come when the words don't avail themselves to me, when the thought of getting from Point A to Point B are not only daunting, but seemingly impossible.

To be openly candid with you, this is my first attempt at authoring a book. Over the previous twenty chapters or so, I've had moments where my fingers can't keep up with my mind and my heart – racing to express all that I'm trying to convey before the moment and words are lost. Then, every once in a while, the word fountain stops flowing. Writer's block strikes.

I am forced to be a spectator to my own self-induced misery, unable to bridge the gap from heart to paper.

In those moments, all progress on this project stops.

Which brings us to the subject of this chapter, dear friend (see what I did there – writer's block conquered once again!). There are potential hazards – roadblocks – to beware as you continue along your journey of grief. For some, these roadblocks can prevent them from ever embarking on the grief journey entirely. But for those who are successfully navigating the journey of grief, these roadblocks can stop progress as quickly as writer's block can stop an author in his or her tracks.

What follows are a few examples of roadblocks you might face on your journey of grief. This list is by no means conclusive, but they are ones I've faced at one time or another over my decade-long journey thus far. And to kick it off, I'll start with the biggest and most dangerous roadblock of all.

Unforgiveness

Yep. It's so important, I'm bringing it up here again, even after devoting an entire chapter to it some time ago. I said it before, and I'll say it again: forgiveness needs to be extended *not for the benefit of the other person* but for *your own personal benefit*. Holding on to unforgiveness is like willfully ingesting a guaranteed cancer-causing agent. If you do not extend forgiveness to whomever has wronged you, *it does that person absolutely no harm* while simultaneously exponentially increasing your own anger and pain while bringing a complete halt to your personal journey of grief.

I don't know about you, but the grieving process is already so painful, so difficult; why would anyone want to make it worse?

Doubt

Doubts, if any exist for you, must be faced head on. One of my favorite scriptures of all time states:

"If any of you lacks wisdom, let him ask God, who gives generously to all without reproach, and it will be given him. But let him ask in faith, with no doubting, for the one who doubts is like a wave of the sea that is driven and tossed by the wind."[1]

There are numerous times during your journey of grief where wisdom will come in handy. That certainly has been the case for me. Yet this isn't the part of the scripture I wish to draw your attention to. It is what the Bible says about the individual who has doubt: "he who doubts is like a wave of the sea driven and tossed by the wind." How can you make forward progress on your journey of grief if you are continually tossed about by doubt?

I saw this first-hand in our own experience after Micah's death. After Micah's death, we were given a sum of money by insurance companies. This money, though more than we expected, was far less than any human life is worth. It was enough money, however, to enable me to stop working full-time as I entered nursing school for the two years it would take to obtain my Associate's Degree in Nursing.

One night while walking with Jenna, she allowed herself to open up to me. She said to me, "Sometimes I feel like Micah died because we didn't know how we were going to pay your way through college." She reiterated that she knew that wasn't true, but that it gnawed at her just the same.

I didn't have a response for her right then, but sometime shortly thereafter, after asking God for wisdom, the answer came. I lovingly replied to her question with another question, "Do you think God is so limited that He had to kill our son so that our bills would be taken care of in college?"

We didn't ignore her lingering doubt, a thorn in her heart that would threaten to derail both of our journeys of grief, but faced it head on. When you are faced with the same, you have two choices. Either ignore your doubts and pretend they don't exist (a sure way to weigh yourself down along your journey, eventually stopping it altogether), or search for the answers to your doubts, either in prayer to God, or by any natural means available to you.

Becoming the Lone Ranger

If you were to head off, trekking into some mountain wilderness, would you think it wise to go alone, regardless of how well you packed for the trip? Not me – no way. I'd want a guide, someone who has been there before, or at the very least someone who knows me, cares for me, and looks out for my interests in addition to their own.

As difficult as a mountain wilderness exploration sounds, I believe the journey of grief is *at least* as difficult, if not more so. Please don't accept the mantra that if you simply "pull yourself up by your bootstraps" and trudge forward alone that all will be well. I guarantee you it won't.

Allow others – a close loved one, a friend, your spouse – in on your journey. Allow them to walk with you, to comfort you, to speak wisdom to you, or to simply be by your side. Their strength, their love, and their desire to see you succeed is not only beneficial to you, it is *essential*. Without accountability, without a partner or guide, it is far too easy to lose sight of your journey, to head off the beaten path, or to simply stop altogether and give up.

Seriousness

Okay, I have to admit this one won't necessarily stop you in your tracks. Yet I find it of great enough importance to include it here with the other roadblocks.

Yes, your loved one has died. Yes, it hurts. Yes, life for you very well might be as bleak as you've ever experienced it. But just as I said earlier in this book that it is okay to cry, it is equally important to remember:

It's okay to laugh.

I briefly touched on it at the end of the previous chapter. I've never had such a spiritual experience playing Uno. Our friends (see – no Lone Ranger, right?) with little effort on their parts allowed us to experience laughter in the midst of darkness. Remember earlier references to Ugly Face Cry? Well this was Ugly Face laugh, and it was so desperately needed in that moment, more so than I ever knew.

Obviously I must preach temperance with this. If you laugh and smile all the time, I guarantee you'll find yourself with a one-way ticket to a funny farm. At the very least, it would be very disconcerting to others. I remember once attending a memorial service for an extended family member of a cute girl I wanted to get to know. This family, comprised of believers in Christ, wanted this memorial service to be a celebration of the loved one's life. No problem there. Yet, for the duration of the entire service, as well as the greeting times before and after, many family members were down right jubilant, almost ecstatic with glee that their loved one was with Jesus. These particular family members *never stopped smiling*. Not once. It kind of creeped me out.

Please don't misunderstand me; my intent is not to mock these individuals or question the motives of their hearts. But I distinctly found the entire experience offsetting. And now that I've personally experienced the death of my son, someone so close to me, I can't *imagine* perpetually walking around like I won the lottery.

Just the same, remember – it *is* okay to laugh. A joyful heart is indeed good medicine[2]; in small and repeated doses you will find it to be a salve for your wounds.

The Tar Pit

This last roadblock on my list, though not nearly as destructive as unforgiveness, has the potential to not only stop you on your journey, but very well might suck the life out of you as it does so.

I remember visiting the La Brea tar pits in California as a young child. I knew I was supposed to find the fossilized bones utterly cool and awesome, but instead walked away from there saddened by thought of those helpless animals, struggling to come to the surface, all the while being sucked further more to their doom.

The same holds true of what I like to call the Why/What If/If Only Tar Pit.

I can hear you now, "But Eric, you actually encouraged me to question God in an earlier chapter. Now you're telling me it can *suck the life* out of me?"

Well, um, yep.

You see, questioning God = good. Obsessively questioning the circumstances surrounding your loved one's death = bad. Suck-the-life-out-of-you bad. I've-just-been-turned-into-a-prune-by-vampires, suck-the-life-out-of-you bad.

Do you recall my personal "why" questions I gave as examples back in Chapter 13 – the chapter regarding forgiveness? Here they are again for your reading pleasure (would hate for you to get finger cramps turning the pages; see – I'm watching out for you):

"Why wasn't I walking on the other side of the road, against traffic, where there was a sidewalk?"

"Why didn't I hear the van approaching?"

"Why did Micah have to be the one to take the brunt of the impact? Why not me?"

Can you detect the difference between these "why" questions and the WHY question I asked in Chapter 16 regarding questioning God? That WHY question simply asked, "Why did our Micah have to die?"

The three questions you see above all question specific circumstances surrounding our accident. It is as if they mockingly snicker behind my back, suggesting that if I only did something different, our outcome might have changed. They are evil, painful, *self-accusatory* questions that, if allowed to permeate my brain and heart, will drag me down faster than any natural tar pit could.

The fourth question, however – the reason why I label it the WHY question (all capital letters) – is one that seeks an answer to a bigger question, a deep question of the heart that can only be answered by God Himself, a question that begs for more than an answer, but a *purpose* behind the event.

It is so easy to get trapped in this. For example, if I was a masochist, I could go down this road of reasoning:

If only Jenna and I hadn't walked on the wrong side of the road...

What if we hadn't stopped to look in the empty house moments before...

Why hadn't we continued on to 24th like we usually did, avoiding 16th and the accident entirely...

But where does this road end? Let me tell you: it doesn't. It only continues to far more dangerous territory.

If only we didn't follow my dream to become a nurse and move to Spokane...

If only we had never conceived Micah in the first place...

If only we never met and fell in love...

If only I had never been born...

Roadblocks suck. There's no other way around it. Look for

these and others to crop up along your journey. Then – please, oh, please – deal with them.

As I said before, these roadblocks have shown up on my own personal journey of grief... a journey that only truly began the morning my son took his last breath.

As I awoke on Tuesday morning, the morning that proved to be the final morning of Hell Week, little did I know that the first day of my journey was about to begin.

(Endnotes)

1   James 1:5-6
2   Proverbs 17:22

CHAPTER 22

All the Way Home

TUESDAY, SEPTEMBER 2, 2003

*W*hether from the exhaustion of the day before, the tears induced by the Uno laughter the night before, or simply because God knew what was next – Monday night I slept as I hadn't slept in some time. I slept so soundly, in fact, that it took a while to come back to reality when Jenna gently nudged me awake that Tuesday morning. "Come quickly," she said. "It's time."

Jenna's grandma, Micah's great-grandma "GG," a registered nurse back in the day, was holding Micah's body when his breathing pattern began to change. His eye was no longer open. The neural screams had ceased some time during the night. The time had come. She had someone wake Jenna. Jenna, after seeing everything for herself, came to wake me.

Jenna and I had previously planned the logistics for the moment of Micah's death. I had told her I wanted to play my "Daddy card" – I wanted to be the one to hold Micah when his body shut down. She lovingly agreed. When I walked into the room that morning, whatever haziness fogging my brain from the previous night's deep sleep instantly vanished. I saw Micah – my olive-skinned baby boy – pale and dusky. His breathing was very shallow and rapid. He was cool to the touch. All the horror that played out in the days previous was instantly forgotten. On this morning, I was going to lose my boy – for good.

Sitting comfortably in a chair with Jenna by my side, I held Micah's body. Family and friends surrounded us. Judging by the number of people in the room, and the anticipation in the air, you would've thought a baby was about to be born. God's love and peace surrounded all of us. Playing on the CD player was a Michael W. Smith worship album. For a good couple of hours, this is how the final moments played out.

Everyone was silent. My mind, however, was not. I couldn't help but look at my son and flash back to the first moment I held him the day he was born – the first moment it was just him and me. Jenna had given birth via C-section, and was fast asleep in her bed. I held Micah in my hands, facing him toward me, as my mind, heart and soul filled with wonder. Here was a little boy created by Jenna and me and the very breath of God.

What would his life have in store for him? What would be his passions, his interests? Would he marry – if so, whom, and where was she now? His entire life was laid bare before him...

...then the memories continued to roll. His fondness for airplanes; he and I talking to cows at the Cowboy church; our first Seattle Mariners game; our first Spokane Indians game; his first birthday; him running to us with his eyes closed, knowing we would be there to catch him if he fell; pulling him around our slightly-cramped apartment in a diaper box attached to rope; clapping and dancing to music; eating (and throwing) blocks of cheese; his belly laugh; his electric smile; his tiny hands as they patted my back when he'd hug me...

...and as quickly as the memories rolled, as quickly as his life flashed before my eyes, I was right back in the room again, staring at this shell of what had once been. I asked one final time for a miracle. It was still within God's power to restore our son. Yet somehow I knew that wouldn't be our story – Micah was, and already had been, in heaven.

At 9:05 that morning, Micah breathed his last. I waited for the next breath. It never came. From across the room, Dr. Peter Graves, another incredible intensivist that cared for our son, then said it best:

"He's all the way home."

CHAPTER 23

...a Dream Reclaimed

DERIVING LIFE FROM DEATH

*D*eath is bad.

I said it before – in Chapter 7, "The Elephant" – and I'll say it again. I personally don't subscribe to a belief in such a thing as a "good death." Sure, for some, death can come as a relief from pain and suffering. In cases like ours, death can even bring an end to inner turmoil and agony. Yet I still contend that death in and of itself is bad.

As also stated before, it was never a part of God's original plan for mankind.

Death brings an end to physical life – the physical life of an individual who has the ability to impact others.

Death quite literally marks the final chapter of the story of a loved one's life. How many chapters of life could have been written by Micah, by your loved one, by any given person, if death does not end that story?

Yet as I have also contended, and you have hopefully seen, good things, including life itself, can be derived from death.

Although I am here primarily referring to the figurative, in Micah's case it also refers to the literal. In one of the final of a long list of decisions Jenna and I had to make, we chose to donate tissue, namely Micah's heart valves, upon his death. Two heart valves were donated – one to a boy in Boston, another to a boy in New Mexico. Something *good* came from Micah's death. Two other children had a chance at an extended life on account of our son's death.

Though it didn't lessen our personal pain, it allowed for a sense of gratitude to accompany that pain.

It is for that reason that I have since become an organ and tissue donor (Jenna has been one long before the accident). It is also for that reason that I make my only personally-inspired sales pitch here: please consider becoming an organ and/or tissue donor. I have had the intense privilege of riding the Donate Life Rose Parade float in honor of our son. In that experience I met some of the most inspiring people on the planet – some family members of organ and tissue donors, some organ and tissue recipients – all of whom have in some way physically derived life from someone's death.

Good *can* come from death.

Returning to the figurative, and more importantly to the subject of this book – you... how can you derive life from death?

You do so by doing the things I've outlined in the previous chapters:

— *You face doubt head-on.*
— *You bring someone along with you on the journey.*
— *You laugh along the way.*
— *You embrace the belief that death is not the end.*
— *You yell at God when you hurt.*
— *You ask God the deep and purposeful questions, trusting Him even if no answer is given.*
— *You actively search out the miracles that are all around you, hiding like little Easter eggs, waiting to be discovered.*
— *You forgive, forgive, then forgive some more. Forgive others. Forgive yourself.*
— *You embrace the idea that grief is a process, not a one-time event.*
— *You express your grief.*
— *You cry.*
— *And almost more importantly, you allow yourself to dream again.*

If you do these things, if you actively embark on the journey of grief, you can once again live life. As I said before, your life will *never* be the same again. There exists a hole in which a loved one's life once lived. Yet that life, the life of your loved one, lives on in you if you continue your journey. You carry his or her torch for others to see. Your own life, whatever remains of it, however many chapters are left to be written, will be brightened by your loved one's torch, their memory.

You will be able to live life again – quite possibly more vibrantly than you did prior to your loved one's death.

On a final note, as you might have already gathered, my faith plays a central role in my life. To that effect, there was one more example of life being derived from Micah's death. The following is the text of a card we received sometime in the months immediately after Micah's death. It was written by one of the intensivists who cared for Micah, who walked with us almost every step of the way during our nine-day hospital stay in the Pediatric Intensive Care Unit. The doctor wrote:

> *I think of Micah often – and your family. I was truly blessed by your family. As one of the nurses said a couple of weeks ago, "I've never seen faith in action quite like the Miller family." Taking care of Micah affected the PICU in a profound way. I don't think there was a doctor, nurse or secretary, for that matter, that wasn't changed by the faith, hope and love that they saw demonstrated by your family. May the Lord bless your 2004.*

I do not include this here to "toot our own horn." We have no horn to toot. Truth is, it wasn't just Jenna and me she referred to, but our extended family and friends who stayed with us at the hospital for that week.

I include it to show that somehow, in the midst of the darkest hours of our lives, in the midst of the intense pain and suffering that inherently comes with a dying child, God worked through our tragedy, through our family and friends, to encourage those around us.

What more could we ask for in such a situation?

CHAPTER 24

Epilogue

Our nightmare didn't end the day Micah died. The healing process began, but we still had to transition from grieving for a dying son to grieving for a dead son. Despite their similarities, there is a world of difference between the two.

After Micah's death was pronounced, family and friends took time to say their final good-byes. The vigil that had been kept since Micah was removed from life-support officially came to an end when I laid his body back into the hospital bed, some 72 hours after it began. Jenna and I were the last of family and friends to leave the room. Despite knowing he was dead, Jenna couldn't leave the room unless she knew someone was in there – she didn't want his body to be "alone." Chaplain John Brewer, an angel of the Lord who walked with us many nights through this horrible ordeal, was the one left with the body when we finally turned and walked out of the hospital – without our son.

It is difficult to describe how odd it is to physically exit a building, knowing your son's body is still within, and knowing you are not coming back for it. For the sixteen months prior to that moment, Micah went with us everywhere. He had not aged enough to attend preschool, so there were very few breaks from him in the physical sense. From the moment of his birth we knew we were charged with caring for him in his entirety, for changing almost every diaper, for feeding, loving, and holding him; we took very seriously our roles and responsibilities in his life. To then be, far too prematurely, in a sense "released" from this charge... it felt completely alien – and wrong. Micah would no longer go with us wherever we went. We no longer would have his well-being to watch out for. It was a transition I was in no way prepared to take on.

We were parents forcibly and unwillingly turned non-parents.

As we well know from experience, and as we've read in various books about grief, everyone reacts to grief differently. When a child dies, some families keep the child's room intact – some down to the last detail. Other families, like ours, begin to take everything down right away. Please don't misunderstand me – we didn't want to forget about Micah or try to erase him from our lives. We simply couldn't deal with seeing his crib in our dining room, his toys around the apartment, or his high-chair against the wall. His pictures stayed up – those would certainly not come down. But everything else had to go or be put in storage.

With the assistance of friends and family, we started the cleaning process the very night we came home from the hospital, and had it completed by the next day. My back pain, originally caused by the accident that took Micah's life but practically forgotten during the previous week, had come back full force. I couldn't do much to help move heavy things – but I did what I could. It would be awhile before I could make an appointment and see a chiropractor for what amounted to little more than soft-tissue damage.

The rest of the week was a blur. Micah's memorial service was to be held on Saturday, September 6th, 2003 – Micah's 17-month "birthday." There was much to prepare. We dealt with the awful task of having our son's body cremated. We made posters filled with pictures from his life. Details had to be arranged.

Ultimately, Micah's service was beautiful. We had as many guests from the Seattle area as we had from our home church here in Spokane – a few hundred or so. The loving support was overwhelming in a good way, and altogether embraced. To be truthful, it was incredibly healing for me to see so many people from all parts of my life, of Jenna's life, from our many years in the Seattle area and from our one year in the Spokane area, come together to celebrate one tiny little life. I am still so thankful to this day for all that attended, remembered individually or not.

After the service, we traveled to Tacoma, Washington to bury Micah's remains. Jenna's grandmother offered to have his remains buried on her family plot in a Catholic cemetery. We agreed, and the graveside service was held, rather anticlimactically, on Tuesday, September 9th, 2003.

Life then had to start getting back to "normal." My employer at the time, Powder Basin Associates, had been beyond gracious with the amount of paid time they gave me – they told me to come back when I was ready, and not a moment sooner. They even went so far as to take up a collection for Jenna and me, *and* agreed to match that collection dollar-for-dollar. Despite their generous offer, I returned to work within a few days of burying Micah.

How do you start life over again after something so jarring, so out of place occurs in an otherwise "normal" everyday life? Come to find out, one day at a time. I was scheduled to start the first Anatomy and Physiology class – a prerequisite class for entrance into the nursing course – that fall quarter. This class was beyond difficult to get into, so I felt I owed it to myself, my scholarship, and my wife to continue on as I had before. I attended one night of class. After hearing that we would cover the neurology unit (including the functions of the brain and spine) that quarter, coupled with the sheer difficulty of concentrating on my studies, I decided to withdraw from school indefinitely until I felt I was ready to come back. I made this decision assuming that I would lose both scholarship money and my position on waiting lists to get into this highly sought-after class. The Lord proved me wrong; the college informed me that they would hold my position in the class as well as all the scholarship money until I returned, whenever that may be.

During the break, we did not immediately join a grief group or receive grief counseling of any sort. Instead, Jenna and I realized we needed to focus on each other. We had heard the alarming statistic that over 80% of married couples who experience the death of a child file for divorce. Having already both come from divorced families, we determined long ago that divorce would never be an option for us. Now we had to work even harder, with the Lord's help, to make sure that didn't happen. We enrolled in a marriage course in our church, one that was kicked off by a marriage retreat. Those decisions helped lay a foundation on which we could rebuild our life.

The break from my studies lasted the entirety of that fall quarter, and then extended to include winter quarter. I came back spring quarter of 2004 ready to face whatever demons needed to be faced to succeed. I never looked back. I graduated with my Associates Degree in Nursing in December of 2006.

Shortly after Micah's death, Jenna and I broached the subject of having more children. We always talked about having more than one, and had, before the accident, coincidentally planned on trying to conceive a second child that fall. At first, Micah's death changed all of that. We didn't know whether we could handle the pain of possibly losing another child. It took only approximately one month before we realized that we weren't getting any younger, that we did indeed want to have more children, and that by having a child, we would be forced to face things that we would eventually have to face anyway. Owen was conceived shortly thereafter. Later came

Amelia. Later still – Peyton. And last but not least, God was kind enough to give us Ava as well. The Lord has richly blessed us many times over, so much so that I will at times joke with others, stating that we over-compensated for the loss of Micah. However, this couldn't be further from the truth. In fact, whenever anyone asks me how many children we have, I respond, "Five – one in heaven and four on earth."

As I mentioned before, the nightmare hadn't ended with Micah's death. There was still much to deal with in the months to come:

— I often went to sleep at night with fears of being taken to court on the account that we withheld life-support from Micah. Despite knowing our decision was the right one, for the reasons mentioned in the previous chapters, I had nagging fears that someone in the general public wouldn't see it that way. My fears were irrational at best, but they were nevertheless very real to me, regardless.

— Compounding those fears was the rise to prominence of the Terri Schiavo case. I won't go into the details of the case here – that's why God and Al Gore created the internet – but it weighed on me heavily. Not once have we ever doubted our decision – not even during those difficult times.

— Jenna, having been raised in churches that equate suffering and death with sin and wrongdoing, had a difficult time not correlating Micah's death with something she had done wrong, or some sin she had committed. She knew in her head that it was silly, but her heart, her years of training, told her otherwise.

— Dealing with an "if only"... Shortly before Micah and I

were hit from behind by the van, I complained of a sore back (Micah was in a carrier on my back during our walk). Jenna offered to take Micah for the remainder of the walk. If I had agreed to that, she and Micah would be safe, and it would have only been me who was hit. Because Micah was on my back, his head took the brunt of the impact; if he was not on my back at that moment, I likely would have been the one to die (which the father in me would rather have had happen). That was a major "if only" for me until Jenna explained that of the two of us (Micah and me), she would rather have me. Sure, Micah was a product of our love for one another, but I am her husband, and as much as she loved Micah, she loves me more – as God intended. This truth has only been compounded over the years, as I watch four other lives birthed from our union that would not be in existence if it had been I who was killed.

This was just a sample of the things we have had to deal with after Micah's death. Be rest assured, God continues to heal us over time, even now, ten years later. We aren't completely healed yet – nor shall we ever be. As I've stated before, despite what some might think or believe, you can't possibly be "completely healed" from the loss of a loved one. But through this process we have learned the value of forgiveness, of love, and of leaning on Him.

As of this writing, we live what most people would describe as a "normal" life. We deal with the day-to-day joys and frustrations of raising four children aged 4 to 9. I work full-time in my occupation as a registered nurse. We go to church. We watch movies and TV shows. We have hobbies. We eat out at restaurants. We even at times get caught up in the ever-increasing fast-paced life of an average American family.

But the effects of those events that transpired now ten years ago still linger. We struggle with avoiding being over-protective of our children. Jenna worries any time a child bonks his or her head. I'm more apt to call in sick at work if one of our kids is sick at home. If we purchase gifts in advance for a birthday or Christmas, it is difficult to not give those gifts right away on account of not knowing *definitively* if our children will live to see their next birthday or Christmas. We want to spend almost every waking moment with each other and with our children – sometimes to a fault. We don't want to waste opportunities we have to spend time with each other. We simply never know when those opportunities might be our last.

Often times people ask us about the people who hit us. Was the driver drunk? Was he speeding? Nope and nope. Truth is, the family that hit us was very similar in age and circumstance – they, a married couple, about our age, with a daughter, about Micah's age. They visited us in the hospital once when Micah's prognosis still looked good. I kept in touch with the husband, the driver of the van, all the way up until Micah's memorial service. I ministered to him the best I could. As much pain and suffering as we experienced, I couldn't imagine the pain and suffering they, and he in particular, experienced. I certainly would not have wanted our roles to be reversed. I invited him to come to the memorial service – under promise that I wouldn't single him out in any way – so that he might have closure to his own personal hell. He and his wife did come – I caught a glimpse of him once at the end of the service and nodded his way. He returned a nod in kind. It was the last time I ever saw either of them.

I pray for them to this day when I think about them. I pray for their daughter, now at an age very close to what Micah would be. Jenna and I have both been angry with them at times throughout the last ten years – more so shortly after Micah's death and in the couple years that followed – but God has always been so gracious with us. How can we not extend that same grace to them and others?

On that note of grace, I'll end this book. It is our hope and desire that you may be ministered to, at least in some small way, by our retelling of the events surrounding Hell Week.

This has been a most difficult endeavor. I've had to ask Jenna questions to make sure my memory isn't screwy; she has proofed each chapter, forcing her to relive the details of that week. I've relived the entire week myself, delving deeper into memories I most often keep hidden within me under lock and key. I've shed more tears, sometimes sobbing at my desk, than I have shed in a long time. I've had interrupted sleeping patterns while writing this – as if there was a wound that hadn't been opened for years. It hurts like hell to open it back up, but the ultimate result is more and more healing.

But more importantly, if there is any person whose life can be positively impacted by these accounts, then this endeavor has been more than worth whatever pain and difficulties I have personally experienced.

If that is you... if you care to share with us your own personal story, your own personal journey, feel free to contact us. You can email us at:

myjourney@fivearrowbooks.com

Or you can write us at:

> Eric and Jenna Miller
> Five Arrow Books
> PO Box 424
> Veradale, WA 99037

If you were in any way encouraged or uplifted by the content of this book and decide you would like more encouraging content emailed to you on a regular basis, please visit our website at www.fivearrowbooks.com and use the subscription form at the bottom of the website. You will receive regularly scheduled editions of Target Practice, our humble little newsletter that aims to bring encouragement to your day.

May you find health, healing, and life on your journey of grief.

May you find that your dreams can be reclaimed.

And most importantly, may the Lord Jesus Christ bless you and keep you.

APPENDIX A

Photographs

The illustrations drawn by our then 5-year-old Amelia, depicting her feelings about the death of the newly acquired family cat, as referenced in Chapter 11.

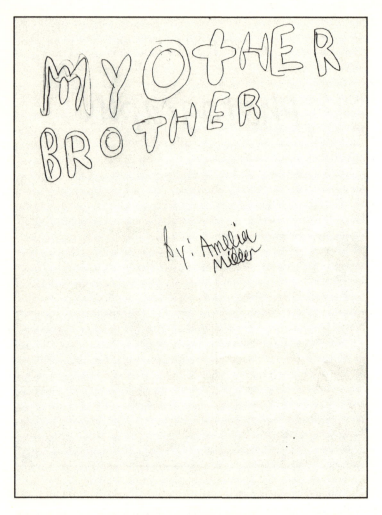

The artist, at it again. 6-year-old Amelia's spontaneous drawing of "her other brother." Micah is not discussed often in our
home (usually only around his birthday and the dates of the

accident and his death). Every once in a while, the kids surprise us with discussions (and in Amelia's case, drawings) such as this.

Micah and I, only six days prior to the accident.

The Miller Family – August 2013

Who knows what's in store for any of us.
Praying for you and every step of your journey.

APPENDIX B

So Close to Grief

As I've stated before, this book was written over the past ten years. A majority of the practical "how-to" chapters were written within the last year.

Back in Chapter 11, I brought up how important it is to express your grief using the gifts you've been given, further referencing my ability and/or desire to write. It wasn't until the eleventh hour of this book's publication process, however, that I recalled a few pieces I wrote in the time immediately following Micah's death. After a little search, I found those writings, and decided it might be a blessing to some of you readers to include them here. (My graphic artist is likely to have a fit... actually, he's a great guy; besides, he'll get paid extra to include them anyway!)

So without further ado, I present to you one final parting gift. Four of these five writings were written within four months of Micah's death. The fifth came just after a year. All of which are raw, possibly giving you a glimpse into the heart of a newly grieving father. (Please note that they are all unedited; I preserved them all the exact way I wrote them years ago, grammatically incorrect warts and all.)

Lil Imitator

September 24-25, 2003

Let me tell you about our son. Micah Anthony Martin Miller was arguably the most adorable little boy you could ever lay eyes on. He had his mother's rich brown hair, round cheeks, and beautiful olive skin (albeit considered handsome on a little boy). His deep brown eyes didn't look *at* you; they looked *into* you. His stature, slender for his age, enabled him to crawl, walk, and run with ease. By the time he learned how to walk, it was one of his favorite things to do. His independent spirit, coupled with his desire to help us out, caused him to prefer pushing strollers and shopping carts to sitting in them. With great excitement he spoke words such as "adah" (airplane), "bay-bah" (baseball), "tuh" (truck), and "bumpa" (grandpa). Other favorite activities included clapping and dancing to music, laughing, talking to cows, climbing stairs on his own, showing off his toys to visiting friends and family, running toward us with his eyes closed, and patting our backs when he hugged us.

We miss him.

A lot.

Reflecting on his life in light of our love for Christ, however, leads me to wonder: Can a 16-month-old child imitate God? After all, the Bible exhorts us to be "imitators of God". In the midst of his simplistic, childhood life, did my son imitate God? After pondering this question for quite some time, I come to one simple answer: let his life speak for itself.

Micah taught us how to love someone unconditionally. It didn't matter what he did; we loved him for who he was.

Even more importantly, he taught us how to *serve* unconditionally. As a baby, hungry for milk, there was no chance for negotiations; he needed food, and he needed it *at that moment*. We were taught how to serve others when we didn't feel like serving anyone.

Furthermore, his joy was contagious. In the midst of the darkest moments of life, Micah could eradicate the darkness simply by flashing one of his electric smiles.

Finally, and most importantly to me: Micah died in my place. He was in a child carrier on my back the day we were hit from behind by a van. Had he have been on my wife's back, I wouldn't be here to write this.

So you tell me: Can a 16-month-old imitate God?

"Therefore be imitators of God, as beloved children."
EPHESIANS 5:1 (ESV)

Ironies (Surrounding Micah's Death)

November 11, 2003

— When Jenna and I first got married, we wanted to wait about five years before having children. At the time of this writing, we are approaching four years of marriage; in that time, we have had a child and lost that child. So much for our plans…

— In the four years we have been married, and the two years of dating before that, I have always walked between my wife and traffic. A pastor of ours suggested this idea to my peers and me. I often thought upon it as being nothing more than chivalrous – much akin to opening doors, etc. On the day of the accident, I was doing that very thing when a van hit my son and I – missing my wife completely, even though we had just been walking side-by-side.

— August 24th, 2001 was the date we found out Jenna was pregnant with Micah. August 24th, 2003 was the day of the accident.

— September 6th, 2003 was the date of Micah's memorial service. It happened to be his "17-month" birthday.

— September 7th, 2002 was the day we packed all of our belongings into one truck and moved from the Seattle area to the Spokane area. On September 7th, 2003, we were moving Micah's stuff out of our apartment.

— Several months before the accident, we purchased a license plate bracket that glorified God in some way, so as to proclaim Christ and curb bad driving habits in one swoop. Originally intending to proclaim Christ's Second Coming, it has since taken on a difficult double meaning. The license plate bracket is still on our car and reads, "WE CAN'T WAIT TO... SEE HIM AGAIN".

— Finally, and what I find most ironic... Micah could very well be currently talking with authors of the Bible he was never old enough to read.

Still Waiting

January 7, 2004

Waiting is an integral part of modern society. A day doesn't go by without the need to wait for something. Think about it. We wait for red lights to turn green. We wait in line at the local post office, grocery store, or bank. We wait for our food to cook. We wait for our favorite television show to come on. Some wait for the "new release" CD, DVD, or video game. Others wait for the release of the latest novel in their favorite series. We wait for our turn at the bowling alley, for our "turn to be seated" at the restaurant, and for popcorn and soda at the movie theater.

My wife and I recently experienced this last example of waiting. Ironically, we waited in line to purchase food that was consumed by the beginning of the movie. However, it was the end of the movie that inspired this writing. At the end of this movie, as one of the heroes returned home, his young daughter ran out of his house to greet him with as large of a hug as she could muster. Shortly after receiving her in his arms, the hero's wife came out of the house holding their youngest son. The four family members then proceeded to hug one another, grateful for the return of the father.

That's when it hit me. That vision of the father's entire family – together, complete, and hugging one another – won't ever happen for me on this side of heaven. The scene hit so close to home because, at the time of this writing, my wife and I are expecting our second child. Our first was taken from us, in our human-minded and limited opinion, far too early. He is enjoying the company of Christ Himself, of heaven in all its glory, and of others gone before us.

So we wait. I wait. I wait for the day when our family will be whole again. Please don't misunderstand me – we thoroughly look forward to the arrival of the newest Miller. But something's missing – namely, Micah. When he died, a part of us died with him. Despite the perfect comfort that Our Lord provides, our lives have forever been changed.

So we wait. When my wife gives birth to Baby Miller Number Two, we will love him or her with everything we have. If and when the Good Lord provides children beyond that, we will love them with every fiber of our beings as well. We continue to love one another – even more so now, I think. And in addition to all this, we continue to love those around us – our family and friends – who make life more fulfilling by choosing to be a part of our lives. Yet, in all the directions our love can be sent, there is one direction from which it can never be sent back – from Micah. Not yet, anyway.

So we wait. We will wait through the ups and downs of life. We will wait through future joy and future pain. We will wait through whatever life may bring.

We members of the Miller family simply have the privilege of experiencing life to its fullest on both sides of this veil we call "death." And someday, praise be to God, the waiting will be over.

Holding My Son

December 15, 2004

I remember it like it was yesterday. I held you in my arms shortly after birth. We were awash in the glow of the lamp that was between Mommy and us; she asleep in her bed, us sitting comfortably in our chair. You were so small, seemingly so fragile. As I sat there, holding you, staring at you, I couldn't help but soak you in. "You are my firstborn, my son," I pondered. "We will do everything within our power to raise you, guide you, nurture you and protect you. You are such a blessing, and we could not be more thankful for you!"

But that was 16 long months ago. Now I hold you, your body still so much smaller than mine, still in need of such protection. But what protection do I have to offer you from death? There is none. In but a few short moments, you will breathe your last. Too soon! It was not supposed to happen this way! I am your father; you are my son. You are supposed to bury me! You are supposed to hold *my* hand as I pass from this world, not I yours!

And such adorable hands you have. Your hands... the hands that would grab hold of my hair when you sat on my shoulders; the hands that patted my back when I hugged you and held you; the hands that caressed my cheeks as I laid you to sleep; the hands that would toss blocks of cheese over your shoulder as you "ate".

But now they are motionless... folded on your belly instead of patting it... as cold and still as a winter's night. How I long for them to reach out and embrace me! If only you could grab my hair one more time!

And your rich brown hair – you had so much of it – even from the day you were born! You had to get your first haircut at six weeks of age. Wasn't that something? It looked exactly like Mommy's, but acted exactly like mine – sticking straight up out of your head like a giant field of dark brown wheat.

But now, cut so short, much of it is shaved entirely, exposing the bolt protruding from your head. If only you would awake! Then it could be allowed to continue to grow, making you look like a little boy again, restoring those fields of wheat on your tiny head.

Your precious head... How we strived to protect it from harm, to support it when you could not yet support it yourself.

But now, what can be done? How can I stop the brain matter from dying, even as I hold you now? How I wish it were *my* head that went through that windshield first, bearing the brunt of an accident that we could not foresee. If only I had seen it coming. If only I had turned around to see with my own eyes the horror that sped toward us, in hopes that I could have prevented it. If only I looked and saw...

Oh, and your eyes! A brown in which we could easily get lost. So expressive, so full of life and light and wonderment! I'm sure you would have melted the hearts of many a lady!

But now, locked up behind the wall of your eyelids, I can gaze at them no more. Maybe it is better that way. I am sure they would be as empty and transparent as they have been the last few days. But could I not steal one more glimpse? Could you not open them one more time, as if to say that you are going to be okay? Could they not open again, to do as they had throughout your life, and speak volumes without saying a word?

And what about saying a word? Can you not open your mouth again, as you did before? Through it you drew breath. From it you spoke – warming my heart by saying my name, "Dah-DEE", every time I came home from work. Using it to give us your patented "open mouth kiss", or blowing on Mommy's belly until you had us laughing so hard we could hardly breathe! And how many times did we make sure *you* were breathing? We were ever concerned about the thief named SIDS, always making sure that as you slept, you breathed.

But now, I barely feel your short, raspy breaths, as you labor to continue to draw the oxygen in. Your tongue lies swollen in the bed of your mouth, no longer able to say my name, or to give us that open-mouthed kiss. Why? What will we do without your coos, your caws, your squealing as you ran toward us in pure delight?

Running toward us... your little legs and feet carrying you as fast as you could muster. Such tiny feet! How cute your sandals were on those feet! I remember with great joy how proud we were of you when you first stood on your own – eating bites of my Snickers Blizzard. You were so caught up in asking me for another bite, you simply forgot we stopped holding you up!

But now, holding you in my arms, they have no life of their own. They are but dead weights at the end of a body waiting to die. So cold to the touch... How I wish I could find socks or booties to warm them! If only they could be used to walk you out of this dreadful room, out of this hospital, out into normal life again – with <u>us</u>!

Oh, God! Will you not restore my son? It's not too late! He still breathes the breath of man; will you impart to him the breath of life?

Please, God.

Please.

The Best School Ever

January 13-15, 2004

Rachel was so excited for her first day of school. She had been told so many times about how much fun it would be, how much she would enjoy it, and how well she would be liked there. But nothing that anyone had said could have prepared her for what she saw when she got there.

Standing outside the schoolhouse, the first thing she noticed was how *green* all the plants were – the grass, the bushes, the trees – everything was so *alive*. It was as if all the greenery was at its season's peak. Through the trees, seemingly cutting the land in half, there bubbled a creek of running water. Rachel remarked at how clear the water looked. Upon closer examination, it seemed so clear that she could almost imagine there was no water. Clear Creek, as she now called it, ran directly behind the school. And what a school it was! At first glance, it looked like a little old schoolhouse – the kind you may see in a small town or children's book. However, though the school was indeed red, and definitely had the feel of an old schoolhouse, it was *far* from old. The red exterior wasn't just red; it was deep red – a dark, deep, and rich red. The color stood out even more thanks to the fact the schoolhouse was spotless. It looked as if someone had cleaned it from top to bottom, then bottom to top again. Rachel's eyes then darted to the bell hanging from the very top of the schoolhouse roof. It looked to her as if it were made of pure gold. She was sure that when that bell was rung, everyone would hear it for miles.

After thoroughly soaking up her surroundings, Rachel decided it was time to go inside. If everything outside the schoolhouse was this magnificent, she thought, she could only imagine what it was like inside! Before she had a chance to open the door, she noticed a sign posted on it. It read:

WELCOME! THIS SCHOOL IS FOR ALL
CHILDREN 7 YEARS OF AGE AND YOUNGER.
COME ON IN – SOMEONE WILL GREET
YOU SHORTLY!

As she opened the door, her eyes and ears immediately absorbed the sounds of children laughing, talking, giggling and squealing. The sounds, as many as they were, were not chaotic, as you or I would expect. They were harmonious – like music to her ears. In fact, behind the squeals, giggles and laughter, she could hear music as well. It was faint at first, but sounded louder if she concentrated on it.

Walking into the schoolhouse, she first noticed the children. They were of all colors, varying in height, but she figured all to be about her age. Some were running around playing tag. Others were drawing pictures, playing games, or listening to the music she had previously detected. It was then that she spotted one boy in particular – off by a wall with a couple of friends. This boy and his friends paid close attention to the music, tapping their toes, singing, and generally enjoying themselves. Although she could not quite make out where the music came from, there was no denying the boy's love for it. His brown hair seemingly bobbed in time with the music as he enthusiastically clapped his hands, encouraging his friends to do the same. He had just about broke into dancing when he looked up and caught Rachel's gaze with his own. His beautiful brown eyes looked at her as though he knew who she was and why she was there.

"Hi Rachel – how are you?" shouted the boy as he approached her with arms open, ready to give her a hug. Before she could respond, the boy embraced her and said, "Welcome! You're new here, aren't you? Shall I show you around?" With a nod of her head, the boy introduced her one-by-one to many of their classmates. Every classmate she was introduced to greeted her differently, but all with such warmth and care that it made her feel as if she never wanted to leave.

"Rachel, this is Elizabeth," the boy began earnestly. "We like to call her 'Hero' because she saved her younger sister from drowning!"

"Wow," she exhaled. "I never met a hero before!"

"And this here is Hope and Gabriel. They're brother and sister, you know. They both used to be really sick – but they're feeling better than ever now!"

"Oooh – follow me over here," exclaimed the boy as he took her to another part of the room. "I'd like you to meet Greg..."

"Hey, is he your brother? You guys look a lot alike."

"No, but we have been asked that before. I think it's just because we have a lot in common."

The boy continued to introduce her to other classmates. He did so with such excitement and enthusiasm that Rachel believed it would only take a few minutes to meet everyone in the room. Yet, strangely enough, every time she was introduced to someone, she instantly felt as if she had known them forever.

"Ashlee, this is Rachel. Rachel, Ashlee. Ashlee is our resident artist. He loves to draw and paint!"

Before Rachel's guide could introduce her to the next classmate, a boy bumped into them with enough force to knock Rachel down. "I'm sorry about that," said the running boy, as he reached down to help her up. "I didn't mean to knock you over – I just got a little carried away."

"That's okay," she smiled. "No harm done."

"This is Joseph," Rachel's guide jumped in. "We like to call him 'Skip.'"

"Skip?" asked Rachel.

"Yah. He used to be in a wheelchair. But now he doesn't have to. That's why he's usually the first to start a game of 'Tag' around here!"

"I see," she said as she caught the glance of another girl near her. "Who is that?"

"Oh," said the boy. "This is Gabrielle. She's our preacher girl. She loves to talk about Jesus any chance she gets!"

"Pleasure to meet you," Rachel said.

"The pleasure's all mine," replied Gabrielle. "I would introduce you to my brother, but he's off playing 'Red Rover' with some of his friends."

"That's okay. It was nice meeting you, though!"

"Nice meeting you too!" Gabrielle replied, blowing her a kiss as she walked away.

Suddenly the sweet sound of a bell being rung was heard throughout the schoolhouse. Rachel immediately knew what it was: the golden bell she saw earlier. "That really does sound like it could be heard for miles," she said to herself.

"We should sit down now," the boy instructed. "That was our five minute warning bell."

Rachel followed the boy to one of the rows of ornately decorated school desks. Each desk was decorated uniquely; like fingerprints and snowflakes, no two desks looked exactly alike. The two children sat next to each other in the front row, very near to the right aisle of the schoolhouse. Rachel watched as the other children she had met filed neatly into their respective desks. Each desk appeared to her as if it had been custom decorated just for the child sitting in it.

"I don't quite get it," Rachel said. "Why aren't there more students here? I thought there would be many more."

"Oh, there are. We get new students all the time – even during class! You see, there are many different schools like this around here. In fact, here comes another new student now!"

Rachel turned around to notice a young girl, about her age and size, enter through the same door she had moments before. This girl had blonde hair down to her back, her eyes were wide with wonder, and her mouth wore a smile so big that Rachel thought it might take over her entire face if she smiled any bigger. Another student greeted the girl, and the two sat down together, talking about a great many things.

Then suddenly, feeling as if she had been very rude, Rachel turned to the boy and said, "Please accept my apologies. I was so excited to be here that I forgot to ask: what's your name?"

The boy looked at her again with his deep brown eyes and said, "My name's Micah. But around here, they call me Angelboy."

"Well thank you for showing me around, Micah. If it's not too much to ask, can I bother you with one more question?"

"Absolutely. It's no bother. What do you want to know?"

"Well, I was wondering... Do you think our parents miss us? I mean, I miss my mommy and daddy so much!"

"I know. I do too. We all do. But as far as our parents missing us is concerned, I'm sure they do. But... But if they only knew what it was like here..." Micah's words and thoughts trailed off to memories of his parents and his time with them.

"Yah, I'm sure our parents miss us," he continued. "However, do you remember when you were escorted here to the school? He said something to you. Do you remember what that was?"

"Of course I do!" she exclaimed. "He said, 'Time doesn't work for us like it does for them.'"

"You see, Rachel, the good news is that your parents will be here soon. Mine too! All of our parents will be here before you know it. And until then, there is so much to enjoy here!"

"I'm so excited! I can't wait for them to see what we're doing now! I can't wait for them to see it all – the desks, the schoolhouse, the music, the running, the smiles, the laughter... This is the best school ever!"

"Well, actually, it's the best *preschool* ever."

"Preschool? But there are kids here ages birth through seven years old! Don't the older kids think that's silly?"

"Most certainly not! They're proud of it! Teacher always starts the class off by saying..."

Before Micah could finish his sentence, the class collectively quieted down.

"Teacher's here!" Micah exclaimed with a sparkle in his eyes.

Rachel could hardly believe it! She recognized His face – He was the One who escorted her to the school! From the moment she met Him, she felt as though she truly knew Him, just as she was also known. Before she could say His name, He said:

"Welcome, My children, to the best preschool ever – Heaven's Preschool!"

Author's note: this is not a biblically accurate account of what happens to our children when they enter heaven. This is a product of the author's imagination. All names used in this story are actual names of children who died, all of varying ages (one miscarriage), children of friends and acquaintances of ours.

ACKNOWLEDGMENTS

They say it takes a village to raise a child, and I firmly believe it takes an equally large village to write a book. I must admit something to you right away: this is one of my favorite sections of any book. After reading an incredibly powerful book, fiction or non-fiction, I take great satisfaction in reading about the people who helped bring that book to fruition. How much more so to now write my own acknowledgements! (Besides, it also admittedly makes me feel like a celebrity receiving some grand award.) Seriously, though, I am confident this book would not be what it is, let alone exist, if not for the people on this list. And by no means is this list exhaustive; if I thanked everyone I want to thank, you would hold in your hands a slightly more entertaining version of a phone book. The following expressions of gratitude are written in no particular order, except for the first:

You, the reader. You are my muse, the reason why I bothered to take the initial steps of my journey all over again. Reliving Hell Week wasn't fun, but if it in any way changed your life, it was worth it. Whether or not I know you, please know that I keep you in my prayers.

Jesus Christ, my Lord and Savior. If not for You, it is very possible I could still be found curled in a ball on my couch, barely able to function.

My dear Jenna, my "first reader." I'd say you are the wind beneath my wings, but by doing so would simultaneously risk a lawsuit from the music industry and/or throwing up a little bit in my mouth (great song; but I'm okay with not ever hearing it again). Regardless, thank you for believing in me and for inspiring me to keep pressing forward. Hmm. Guess you are the wind beneath my wings after all.

Kristi Heilig and Bethany Fitzgerald, editors extraordinaire. You stink. Like smelly cheese. But I love you anyway. (You loved this temporary acknowledgment enough in the draft, I decided to keep it.) But seriously... Though I am separated by a combined 4,700 miles from you both, you managed to bridge that gap, living right inside my heart and mind over this past year. You have exponentially improved an average-at-best author. I cannot thank you enough. Perhaps one day my family can physically overcome those aforementioned miles, take a great American road trip, and thank you and your families in person. Thank you Kristi for setting aside any initial misgivings and concerns about reading such a sensitive subject matter; your ability to do so benefited this work tremendously. As I briefly tutored you so many years ago, I now feel as if you have returned the favor one-hundred fold. And thank you Bethany for finally taking one of my best friends "off the market." Our high school selves would have laughed in our faces if we told them we found such amazing God-fearing women.

Monya Mollohan. As one of the only other people to read this thing cover-to-cover pre-publication, your words of encouragement were both timely and encouraging. Thank you for calling me author long before I'd call myself one.

Jerry and Michelle Dorris, and the entire team at author-support.com. Your cover and interior design solutions are second to none. Thank you for rescuing me from my self-induced InDesign nightmare. More than that, thank you for allowing the Lord to shine through you and your work.

Saralynn Downing, long-distance friend, former intern, slave. Despite the miles and the years, you took the imprint that was in my heart and directly put it to paper. I will forever be your grateful slavedriver. INXS forever!

Tiffany Vakaloloma at Inspirations by Tiffany. If anyone ever has to get shot, I hope you are the one doing the shooting. Thank you for your excellent photography, making me presentable by causing others to overlook the multiple-children-stress-wrinkles and night shift skin translucency inherently found in my face.

Dr. David Clarke, and by extension, Dr. Ward and Cherie Buckingham and Randy Wells. This chain of connections, originating with Mr. Wells, led me to a man who served as a mentor for me during this authorship adventure. Thank you Randy, for always asking about "that book of yours." Your encouragement has been vital to this book's success. Speaking of success, Drs. Clarke and Buckingham, if this book is half as successful at improving lives as your efforts toward improving marriages, I will be thankful. May our Lord continue to bless the works of all of your hands.

My childhood bullies. No, seriously. Looks like the torture you put me through was good for something after all. Thank you for personifying Genesis 50:20: "As for you, you meant evil against me, but God meant it for good, to bring it about that many people should be kept alive, as they are today."

All of the friends and family that physically came to be with us during Hell Week and during Micah's memorial service. Whether you came from near or far, we can still feel your hugs and support over a decade later. Especially to Norman, Carol, Jonathan, and Jamie Arriola; thank you for coming all the way down from Alaska, and for taking us to a much needed dinner at Outback Steakhouse.

On that note, I'd like to specifically thank my uncle, Tim Moore, for speaking during Micah's memorial service, changing my perspective to see that Micah, maybe more than the rest of us, lived a full life. Your words shot across the sanctuary straight into my heart, reverberating throughout time, comforting me now even as I type this. Love and miss you.

My friends – no – *family* at the now defunct Powder Basin Associates. You rallied around Jenna and me in ways too innumerable to mention, and far too appreciated for simple words. If "Hell Week" and "The Accident" are to be forever seared upon our hearts, the love and support we felt from each and every one of you who worked there during that time is as well, forever marrying smiles and joy with the ever-fading sadness.

The "Young Marrieds" couples – the Carrillos, Carrolls, Clarks, Coffeys, Davises, Joneses, Piatts, Tritles and Weavers. Your friendship will forever be remembered as something that helped us through those dark days. Thank you for being so incredibly understanding as we watched your children play minus our little Micah, and for your continued acceptance of our bruised and broken selves after the accident. We could have found no better friends than you during those years. We love you dearly.

The doctors and nurses that provided such excellent care of our Micah. Special thanks to Drs. Brutocao, Fry, Graves and Gruber; your expertise, guidance and counsel made our ordeal somewhat easier to bear. And to Kristy, Diana, Broc, and the other nurses whose names we can't recall, thank you for not only providing the best care we could have ever asked for, but for opening my eyes to the values of hospital nursing. I can honestly say without our experience and your influence, I would not be an inpatient nurse today.

To chaplains John Brewer and Clark Peterson. You were with us practically every step of the way. Thank you for being there for my wife while I wasn't entirely myself. Thank you for gently broaching the subject of organ donation. And thank you for loving us; we felt as if you had known us forever despite having not met either of you until the accident caused us to cross paths.

My mother, Cathy Miller. Thank you for sacrificing so much to help make me the man I am today. Looking back, I know now that it certainly wasn't easy for you. One thing I know for sure: if my children are loved as much as you loved Erin and me, I know they'll turn out a-ok. We love and miss you dearly.

My grandmother, Dorothy Miller now Davenport. You provide a standard I have continually striven for – always giving of yourself to benefit others. I have no doubt that when Jesus sees you face-to-face, He will say, "Well done, my good and faithful servant." Thank you for being Jesus on earth to your friends, children, grandchildren, great-grandchildren, and great-great-grandchildren. And thank you for loving me despite my continued success at Hand and Foot.

Dan and Mary Shegrud. Thank you for loving Jesus, loving my family, and loving each other. Thank you for initiating the Micah holding vigil back at the hospital; it means so much to us, even today. And although your visions for Micah House did not come to pass as you thought they would, your ministering hearts continue to bless so many people. Even more than all of this, thank you for being the grandparents to our children that Grandma Dorothy was to me.

Peggy Miller now Gepford. Thank you for spending the night at the hospital with Jenna that first night. And thank you for sharing with us your Micah dream and subsequent planting of "his tree."

My current coworkers, fighting the good fight on the front lines of childhood sickness and disease. Thank you for putting up with my ramblings about wanting to be an author and whatnot, for providing encouragement when needed most (your cartoon clip *still* makes me chuckle, Jana), and for encouraging me when I had to step foot in the PICU again – not as a father, but as a nurse. I pray you never have to care for my children, but if you do, I know they will be in the best of hands.

All the pastors in my life that have had a hand in shaping and molding me. Specifically, Pastor Jack Holt, for introducing me to Jesus some twenty years ago and whose enthusiasm for the Lord knows no bounds. For Pastor Jim Burton, who drove the almost 300 miles to be at our side the night of the accident; we are forever grateful. For Pastors Craig and Cyndi Langhans, who walked most intimately with us during the most difficult of steps on grief's journey (and whose idea it was to offer animal crackers for memorial service communion). And lastly, Pastor Nathan Rector, a man with his priorities in place if ever I saw one. I am thankful for your leadership, vision, and pastor's heart. Good thing – you have an awful lot of big spiritual shoes to fill.

The 2013-2014 Seattle Seahawks. As I write this acknowledgment to you, you are currently holding a league-best 10-1 record, mere hours away from one of the biggest games of the regular season against the incredibly tough Saints. Even if the rest of your season ends in abysmal failure (I hate to be such a pragmatist, but I grew up following Seattle sports teams, after all), you have still provided me opportunity to hope in Seattle sports once again. More than that, you provided much needed weekly distraction during this arduous writing process. Thank you, and may your season's future fair better than any that have come before.

And last but not least, my dearest four living children. Thank you for understanding. For being patient with a mother who at times sees accidents waiting for you around every corner. For carrying the memory of your brother in your hearts. For your sensitivity. For bringing healing to your parents in ways we never imagined possible. And most importantly, for knowing that our love for you knows no bounds. Although the frustrations of daily life sometimes reign supreme, know that we absolutely cherish every single minute we have with you, and wouldn't have it any other way.

An exceptionally effective speaker, presenter, preacher, and teacher, Eric Miller is a happily married father of five – one in heaven and four alive. After a vehicle-pedestrian accident claimed the life of his firstborn son in 2003, Eric has made it his life's mission to minister to others facing hardship and grief after the death of a loved one. A Bachelor's prepared registered nurse certified in pediatric hematology, oncology, hospice and palliative care, Miller supports patients and families fighting the war against cancer. In his spare time, Eric has appeared in newspapers, television commercials, and has been featured not only on the cover of Providence's Heart Beat magazine but was also selected as one of 24 national riders of the 2009 Donate Life Rose Parade float. He resides with his wife in Spokane, Washington, attempting to raise his four living children without losing his sanity in the process.

Made in the USA
Las Vegas, NV
21 February 2023

67897355R00121